Praise for *All in the Same Boat*

"Rennie is a tremendous storyteller and writes in a way that makes you want to keep turning the pages. There were times I felt like I was in the Atlantic on patrol with him. This book is filled with powerful, thought-provoking stories and lessons that can be applied in any industry."

— **Mack Story**, author of the *Blue-Collar Leadership®* series

"This is a terrific read for anyone who is interested in developing and growing as a leader. You will love how Jon recounts stories and lessons learned through the lens of being a nuclear submariner and how they directly translate into maximizing your experiences in business and in life. Jon highlights the ingredients necessary to put in place the right mindset, culture, and systems to get everyone you lead all in the same boat."

— **Larry Widman**, M.D., high-performance psychiatrist and elite mindset coach, co-founder of Performance Mountain, and author of *Max Out Mindset*

"Jon Rennie captures the essence of what is most important for creating healthy cultures and achieving results: People. He does this through masterful storytelling that oscillates between two uniquely different settings, weaving common threads of leadership and lessons that apply to any team or organization. Rennie's humor, authenticity, and personal experiences are very engaging, but his focus on the reader's own learning and application is what makes this book so influential and practical."

— **Jason Wenschlag**, Ed.D., Executive Director of Teaching & Learning, Minnehaha Academy

"Rennie does a masterful job of telling colorful and powerful submarine stories, immediately relating them directly to business applications. Whether you are running a large organization, someone who is intrigued by submarines, or a leader looking to gain additional insights, this is your book."

– **John Gregory Vincent**, retired submarine Command Master Chief and co-founder of The Submarine Way

"Rennie has very cleverly drawn from his experience as a nuclear submariner and uses examples of practices and principles which are directly translatable to your business, or even your personal life. The stories with lessons learned are compelling, making this book both interesting and enjoyable. It is indisputable that the nuggets of leadership advice presented will make you a better leader and enhance the performance of your team."

– **Fred Stuvek Jr.**, former naval officer and author of *It Starts with You*

"This is an incredibly inspiring and interesting story of Jon Rennie's time serving our country as a naval submarine officer and how his experiences helped him become a better leader throughout his career in manufacturing. Rennie shares personal accounts and highlights critically important challenges and solutions that will help any individual – no matter the industry – surface more equipped to lead."

– **Jawad Ahsan**, CFO of Axon and author of *What They Didn't Tell Me*

"Rennie tells inspiring stories from both his time as a submariner and a business leader. Every story conveys important leadership lessons as well as just good human lessons. Among them are how to communicate with clarity, how to build a team that is accountable and bonded, and how to solve problems by running at them rather than away from them. No matter your tenure as a leader, what Jon Rennie shares from a life both below and above the water will prove invaluable."

– **Neal Woodson**, author of *The Uncomplicated Coach*

"Rennie shows us that the leadership lessons he experienced as a young officer are easily transferrable to today's corporate landscape. He eloquently describes leadership stories and experiences serving under the sea and relates them to the successful businesses he has led in his post-Navy career. If you want to become a better leader, this book is for you."

— **Mitchell Boling**, author of *Leading from the Middle: Teachers and Coaches*

"Jon has crafted a fantastic read that seamlessly weaves what we sailors call 'sea stories' from life onboard the *USS Tennessee* with his experience as a leader in industry and business. As you read through his growth as a leader in the Navy and how he transitioned to corporate life and finally his own business, you'll begin to see that leadership is an art, a practice, and a sorely needed skill set. We don't need more bosses. We need better bosses. We need better leaders. In short, what you'll learn is that as leaders, we are all truly in the same boat."

— **Chuck Whitworth**, retired Navy Chief Petty Officer

"Another great leadership book from Jon Rennie. The movie *Titanic* would have had a happy ending if only Rose and Jack had read *All in the Same Boat*!"

— **John Brubaker**, best-selling author of 13 books on leadership performance

"Fantastic! Every chapter encapsulates amazing leadership lessons. How he goes back and forth from a specific experience on the submarine to relating it to his professional experiences in business is superb! I have to say that I wanted to keep reading more. I cannot wait for his next book!"

— **Lou Everett**, co-owner of the Lou Everett Group

"Get ready because this book, with its intense leadership stories and lessons, will grab your attention from the start and keep you vigorously highlighting and taking notes until the very end. Rennie does a tremendous job teaching practical and applicable leadership skills through the eyes of a submarine officer and in all his amazing stories. A book you won't want to put down!"

– **Ronald D. Donnell**, 1st Lt. USAF

"Not your typical leadership book. Its lessons are key ingredients in the antidote for the leadership crisis plaguing companies today. Leveraging the art of storytelling, Rennie eloquently blends lessons learned as a naval officer and industrial business leader into a powerful call to action for both junior and senior leaders. You will finish this book with not only actionable guidance on how to elevate your leadership capacity, but also with a compelling desire to lead with renewed conviction."

– **Max Hourigan**, chief of staff, Nolan Transportation Group

"Rennie charges right into the fire with his new book, *All in the Same Boat*. The book has relatable stories from both the corporate world and submarine service, making it easy to understand difficult leadership concepts. I took away some great lessons in every chapter, thanks to its powerful exercises that made everything actionable for me."

– **Jeff Akin**, former submariner and vice president of the Akin Collective

"The storytelling is intriguing and keeps you turning the page, revealing easy-to-understand principles about how to lead. His lessons in leadership are straightforward and can be applied to whatever team you are leading."

– **Heather Eason**, founder and CEO of SELECT Power Systems

"Jon Rennie exemplifies the abilities to lead under pressure and how to build a high-performing team. Train, test, and execute even deep under water during 'controlled chaos' is front and center in this book. In a high-risk environment, Jon's leadership lessons will make a powerful impact. This book is a must-read!"

— **Robert "Bo" Brabo**, former presidential communications officer for Presidents Bush & Obama and author of *From the Battlefield to the White House to the Boardroom*

"Jon's ability to utilize his experience in the United States Navy on board a nuclear submarine and translate it into practical leadership lessons and advice is unique. The leadership advice Jon provides is applicable to any industry. If you are truly ready to enter the space of servant leadership, this is the book for you."

— **Evan Whitehead**, M.Ed., veteran school district leader, consultant, and speaker

"This book is exactly what business leaders need today. On a submarine, crew members have to confront problems head-on and work them out before they get bigger. There is no escape. They survive by working together to accomplish the mission. This can be done in business as well. Rennie's sea stories bring excellent context to the powerful lessons he articulates. I found this book entertaining, educational, practical, and valuable. I highly recommend it."

— **Christian Espinosa**, author of *The Smartest Person in the Room*

"Through colorful and compelling stories, this book tells one basic truth: Leadership is a people business. If you want to learn how to get the most productivity, creativity, and respect out of your employees, take action today to show your people that you care about and value them. Just like on a submarine, every employee is critical to your success."

— **Pete Havel**, author of *The Arsonist in the Office*

ALL IN THE SAME BOAT

Lead Your Organization Like a Nuclear Submariner

Jon S. Rennie

ALL IN THE SAME BOAT: Lead Your Organization Like a Nuclear Submariner
Jon S. Rennie

First edition published in 2021
by Deck & Conn, LLC
Wake Forest, NC 27587

© 2021 by Jon S. Rennie

All rights reserved. This book or any portion thereof may not be reproduced or used in any manner whatsoever without the express written permission of the author except for the use of brief quotations in articles or book reviews.

Requests for permission should be made in writing to:
Jon S. Rennie
jon@jonsrennie.com

Edited by: Mary Lou Reynolds
Cover and interior design: Daniel Yeager, Nu-Image Design

Printed in the United States of America

Library of Congress Cataloging in Publication Data is available from the author upon request.

ISBN 9798739274977

For more information visit Jon S. Rennie's website:
JonSRennie.com

Contents

Introduction 11

Chapter 1. Run to the Fire 17

Chapter 2. Earn Your Oxygen 41

Chapter 3. Communicate with Precision 69

Chapter 4. Eliminate Failure as an Option 93

Chapter 5. Lead Like You Are All in the Same Boat 127

Chapter 6. Develop a "No Escape" Mindset 165

Chapter 7. Run Your Ship Like a Captain 197

Chapter 8. Celebrate the Tough Times 233

Afterword 273

Introduction

I'll never forget the first time I saw the *USS Tennessee*. She was dry-docked at the Trident Nuclear Submarine Refit Facility in Kings Bay, Georgia, the largest covered dry dock in the Northern hemisphere. In the presence of this enormous building, I immediately felt intimidated by what I was about to do. With my sea bag over my shoulder, I summoned all my courage and entered the colossal space. What I saw took my breath away.

I had just arrived in Kings Bay, fresh out of submarine school, and had flown to southeast Georgia to join the crew for deployment. I was an ensign, the lowest-ranking officer in the military. After four years of studying mechanical engineering and another year and a half of intense nuclear and submarine training, I was finally here. The Navy believed I had enough basic knowledge to be assigned to the fleet.

I had orders to report to the commanding officer of the *USS Tennessee*, and I was excited to put all my training to use. Unlike most technical people, I didn't have a deep love for engineering and viewed engineering school simply as a means to an end. I knew I needed a technical degree to become a submarine officer, so I chose a field of study that would give me the best shot at getting on the boats. It was my dream

Introduction

to serve on a nuclear submarine and I had spent six years preparing for this very moment. I was finally ready. That is, until the first moment I saw the *Tennessee*.

An Ohio-class submarine, the largest in the U.S. fleet, is an impressive sight to behold. At 560 feet in length, these $2 billion warships are nearly the size of two football fields. What's even more striking is to see these boats out of the water. When I entered the dry-dock area, I saw the *Tennessee*. She was larger than I had imagined and everywhere around her was activity. There were countless lines, pipes, and hoses running to and from the boat. Orange grinding sparks and the blue light of arc welders danced on the black hull. There was banging, yelling, alarms, horns, and the roar of generators. The acrid smell of diesel exhaust and welding fumes sat heavy in the air. I could see hundreds of people in and around the dry dock working feverishly to get the *Tennessee* ready for sea. It was a complex cacophony of noises, smells, and views I could barely comprehend.

As I took in this scene, I was awestruck. My training never prepared me for the reality of what was unfolding before me. I was about to take a significant role in this high-stress, fast-paced, and demanding environment; and as I thought about the challenge of leading people in this complex and dangerous world, I suddenly realized – I wasn't ready for this.

Introduction

What I didn't know at the time was that I was heading out on a four-year adventure that would change my life and establish principles of leadership I would rely on for decades. I would learn valuable lessons about people, stress, hardship, teamwork, winning, losing, and the impact one leader can make on an organization. I would discover that observing the interactions of officers and enlisted sailors on a deployed submarine at sea was an excellent place to learn leadership and organizational behavior.

In all, I made seven patrols on the *Tennessee*. I started as an unqualified ensign who could barely find my way around the boat. But by the end of my tour, I was an experienced lieutenant qualified on every watch station. Throughout those four years, I was a leader and served as a division officer in both the engineering and weapons departments. I was responsible for leading sailors in these highly technical areas. Unlike business leadership, submarine leadership was a 24/7 commitment. You couldn't go home at the end of the day or take the weekend off after a rough week. There was no escape from your roles and responsibilities as a leader.

Living and leading on a deployed nuclear submarine at sea was a genuinely unique work experience. When we left port, we operated alone for close to three months. We were hundreds of miles from any support and hundreds of feet below the surface. Our mission was to remain undetected and be ready to launch our missiles if required. We were surrounded on all sides by the pressure of the Atlantic Ocean, an

Introduction

emotionless enemy who could care less whether we lived or died.

The only thing that kept us safe was our fellow crewmates. To accomplish our mission and return safely home to our families, we relied entirely on each other. We had each other's back. There was a shared responsibility and vulnerability. Any mistake by even the most junior sailor could result in the submarine's loss and everyone on it. It didn't matter what your rank was; we were all in it together. We were all in the same boat.

That experience gave me a strong appreciation for people. It helped me understand the critical importance of every person in an organization, regardless of rank. When I entered the business world, I discovered this awareness was a rare trait. Many business leaders I worked with didn't have that same appreciation for employees, especially those in the lower levels of the organization. In contrast, I learned that treating people with respect and tapping into a team's collective wisdom yielded powerful results.

Applying the lessons I learned in the Navy led to success in the business world. In 22 years in corporate America and five years as an entrepreneur, I have successfully led nine different manufacturing businesses, and I credit that success to the extraordinary lessons I learned as a young officer on the *Tennessee*. The purpose of this book is to share those lessons.

INTRODUCTION

This book revolves around eight major themes, and they are taught through both sea stories and business stories. But rest assured, they are mostly explained through sea stories. Readers of my best-selling first book, *I Have the Watch*, said they wanted to hear more about my time under the ocean. This book is the answer to that request. Each chapter contains stories that relate to the theme and are not in any chronological order. I jump around to different points in my naval and work experience to help illustrate the lesson.

Throughout this book you will better understand what life is like on a nuclear submarine. You will learn from my first-hand experiences of the unique challenges we faced on long, isolated patrols with little contact with the outside world. You will understand why we did things a certain way to ensure the success of the mission and eliminate any chance of failure. More importantly, you will discover how these principles translate directly into your organization.

As you get ready to dive into this book, I challenge you to do one thing as you read through the stories in these chapters. Consider each one in the context of your own leadership story. Ask yourself this question: *How can I use these concepts to become a more effective leader in my organization?* I guarantee you will get more out of the book if you are an active reader. At the end of each chapter, you will have a chance to reflect. I provide a summary of the key points, tweetable quotes, and questions for you to ponder. To get the most from the book, take notes and spend

Introduction

some time considering the questions in each chapter.

Finally, let me answer a question that is probably on your mind right now. *Is a submarine considered a ship or a boat?* Although you will see me use both terms in the book, submarines are historically referred to as boats. This is because a boat, in naval terminology, is a vessel launched from a larger ship. The earliest submarines were small and were both launched and supported from larger ships, so they have traditionally been called boats from the earliest days of submarine history.

Are you ready to dive in? Let's get started.

Chapter 1. Run to the Fire

Any fire aboard any vessel can be perilous, but flames, and the noxious smoke and gasses they produce, unleashed within the tight confines and self-contained atmosphere of a submarine present a whole other level of danger for ship and crew.

– Tyler Rogoway, editor of *The War Zone*

Controlled Chaos

The familiar gongs of the general alarm rang through the boat. I was fast asleep but the constant wail of the alarm brought me out of the deep fog. Then I heard it over the ship's speaker, also known as the 1MC: "Fire in the laundry! Fire in the laundry!" Not many things will wake you up faster and get your adrenaline pumping quite like those words, especially on a deployed submarine in the middle of the Atlantic Ocean. I was up in a flash. I didn't need to get dressed. Like most sailors, I slept in my uniform, a set of blue coveralls affectionately known as a "poopy suit." I left my stateroom and headed aft in a sprint.

My assignment during a fire was to run directly to it. I had two objectives: (1) Take charge of firefighting until relieved by the executive officer and (2) establish communications with the control room. I quickly maneuvered my way through the boat's tight spaces, grabbing an EAB along the way. An EAB, or Emergency Air Breathing device, is a face mask with a long hose used for breathing in an emergency. There are manifolds throughout the ship where you can plug in the hose and breathe fresh air. During a fire these masks kept us alive as we fought the flames. Wearing an EAB is known in the submarine community as "sucking rubber." I donned my EAB and quickly made my way to the ship's laundry.

As I reached the missile compartment, I quickly saw the red baseball hats of the drill team. There was no fire this time; it was a drill. Members of the drill team placed an opaque covering over my EAB to simulate the low visibility of heavy smoke. I directed teams to set up fire hoses throughout the compartment and establish communications with the damage control team. A fire drill is controlled chaos, and this drill was no exception. The first responders worked quickly to organize firefighting equipment in the limited visibility, all while keeping the EAB hoses from becoming hopelessly tangled. A sound-powered phone operator set up contact with control and I made my initial reports from the noisy compartment. I smiled as I watched the team operate in the tight quarters because I could see the trained sailors knew precisely what to do. I was just there to oversee our efforts. They had done this hundreds of times.

In short order, we fought the simulated fire until it was out and conditions were safe. We had accomplished our objective by getting the fire out in the allotted time. Our team was good because we trained hard on all potential casualties, but we were exceptionally proficient at firefighting. On this day we proved, once again, that we were ready to handle anything that could happen.

Most people are surprised when I tell them I'm a trained firefighter. They know I served on submarines but they don't know what that means. They are not aware that every member of a submarine crew is trained to fight fires. It is part of our basic submarine training, and there's a good reason for it. A fire on a submarine is one of the most dangerous things that could happen on board. Smoke can quickly fill compartments and asphyxiate sailors. The heat and flames can spread to weapons, volatile materials, and critical systems, creating catastrophic damage. Small fires become big fires. A massive fire can quickly incapacitate the crew and disable the sub, which is precisely what happened to the *Losharik*, a Russian submarine

In July of 2019, a suspected battery malfunction caused a fire to break out on the Russian nuclear special operations submarine *Losharik*. The fire was initially small and Russian reports indicated that it "did not pose a great danger to the crew." The Russian sailors fell back on their training and, like American submariners, they ran to the fire. The Russian submariners put up a valiant fight as the fire eventually engulfed an entire boat section. After the incident, an inspection of the compartment showed sailors had used up all the fire-extinguishing equipment in that section as they fought the fire for more than 40 minutes. In the end, 14 sailors died, as they eventually ran out of breathable air. Their actions, however, saved the rest of the crew and the heavily damaged submarine.

That's why we learned to attack the fire when it was still small and why we trained so hard in firefighting. We also had to learn to fight our natural instincts. Think about it. If a fire occurs in a building, the natural instinct is to run away. It's natural to move away from fire and exit as quickly as possible. You probably have been through fire drills where you work or go to school. The plan is simple on land: Run away from the fire and call in the professionals to handle it. On a submarine at sea, things are different. You can't dial 911. The crew was trained to ignore their instincts to run away from the fire. When a fire breaks out, they run towards it. Every life is at stake when a fire breaks out on board. Getting it extinguished quickly is the primary objective.

This same mindset was applied to solve all types of problems when we were on patrol. If we had an equipment malfunction, a personnel issue, or a potential threat, we aggressively moved toward the trouble to address it. We never allowed a problem to grow because we knew it would have significant consequences for the crew and the mission. We ran toward problems to get them under control quickly.

So you can imagine my surprise when I first entered the business world after the Navy. What I learned is that this kind of mindset is rare. Often in business, problems are ignored or rationalized away. People are worried about their careers, so there is a tendency to move away from anything negative. Small issues are overlooked and are allowed to fester and grow. In the worst cases, these problems grow to the point of pervading the entire organization.

Just like on a submarine, there are some situations in business that, if not addressed immediately, can cause permanent, catastrophic damage. These might include a product failure, a customer complaint, a change in the market landscape, or any number of challenges that businesses face each day. What's different is that many of these business problems aren't seen as significant. They don't inspire the same sense of urgency as a fire. Employees aren't trained on what to do. They aren't inspired to attack problems. In the interest of career preservation, many employees avoid getting involved. People follow their natural instincts and move away from or ignore the problem.

Take, for example, the bankruptcy of RadioShack, the electronics retail chain. Their demise is often referred to as a "slow-motion collapse" because all the warning signs were there. Still, RadioShack's management team did little to attack the problems. They didn't run toward the fire. The market had changed dramatically. Other companies, like Best Buy, were doing a better job at solving technology issues for customers. Walmart and online retailers like Amazon now sold many of the components, wires, and connectors that were once only available from RadioShack. The chain became hopelessly stuck in the past and eventually became the last choice for customers. As a result, stores were empty, employees sat idle, revenues fell, and RadioShack stock lost all of its value.

One thing my firefighting training taught me is that we can't allow a problem to go unchallenged. We put our organizations and our employees at risk through a lack of action, so we must create a culture where employees are encouraged to run toward the fire. Like submarine firefighters, employees must be trained and encouraged to run toward challenges and ignore their natural instincts to move away from or avoid them.

While leadership is the act of influencing a group of people to accomplish a goal, a leader is also responsible for establishing a culture that encourages the right organizational behaviors. A culture of finger-pointing and passing the blame only encourages employees to avoid problems. A workplace where employees are regularly fired or disciplined for honest failures creates a workforce unwilling to take risks. Creating the right culture is just as important as hiring the right team and setting the right objectives. Building this culture starts at the top of the organization.

Battle "E"

I was exhausted but the star-filled skies and warm tropical breezes had me in a good mood. We had been up for days conducting MK48 torpedo proficiency-firing exercises at AUTEC, the U.S. Navy's Atlantic

Undersea Test and Evaluation Center, located near Andros Island in the Bahamas. We were going through an intensive assessment of our war-fighting capabilities and our ability to survive in tactical situations. This test is known as a Tactical Readiness Evaluation. That meant we were either running drills or were at battle stations for 72 hours straight. The Navy had several senior officers on board who were evaluating our every move as a crew. Standing the midwatch as the officer of the deck on the surface was a welcome relief from the constant action. It was just the lookout and me on the bridge, and it was a perfect night in the Caribbean.

We had been on patrol for more than two months before heading south for this evaluation. We had trained hard as a team during this deployment, and we were more than ready to show off our skills. We had practiced our response to every potential casualty and tactical situation so often that it was almost automatic. Each of us knew what to do in every case. When it came to attacking a problem, we were good and we wanted to show that to the senior officers on board.

The truth is, the Navy is very competitive, and each command takes pride in being the absolute best at what they do. Part of the reason for this is simple bragging rights, but it's more than that. Training is all about building the war-fighting capability of a ship so it will be ready for anything. A submarine crew has about 20% turnover every deployment, so new personnel must be integrated into the organization and understand their roles. The only way to do this is with constant exercises and drills.

As it turned out, we were very good. We achieved the highest scores in tactical readiness and casualty response. As a result of this readiness evaluation and several others throughout the past year, the Navy awarded our boat with the Battle Efficiency Award, commonly known as the Battle "E." This designation was significant. It's an award only given to the top command. It showed that the overall readiness of our boat to carry out wartime tasks was the best. The competition for the award was fierce but we came out on top. Each member of the *Tennessee's* crew was presented with the Battle "E" ribbon. It signified to everyone that we were part of an elite team. When it came to preparation and running to the fire, we were among the best in the fleet.

The Navy created a culture that celebrated those who were good at attacking problems. Every organization should do this. For example, in the companies I have led, I routinely stressed that employees should always take care of customers first. If a customer needs a report, has a question, or needs assistance, that should be the first thing you do. With that mindset, the businesses I led have received many awards for outstanding customer service. But more important to me are the dozens of calls and e-mails I received from customers who were extremely happy with how one of our employees dealt with a problem. I make a point to thank these employees personally and discuss it in staff meetings and town hall events. Celebrate the employees who take a relentless approach to address problems before they get out of control. These are your company's heroes.

There is another critical point about firefighting as well, organizations that lack structure and stable processes. In these companies, employees are perpetually putting out fires. Most of the management team move from crisis to crisis. This is an unhealthy organizational situation, and it's not the kind of firefighting I am referring to. It's the leader's job to build a stable, smooth-running business. Needing to run to a fire should always be the exception and not the rule.

Be careful not to ignore the other heroes in your organization also. Some employees keep the fires from ever occurring. These employees consistently do their job effectively and efficiently. They keep the company on course by completing their work on time and in full every day. Their thankless efforts often go unnoticed, but they are the ones who prevent the crises in the first place. Celebrate them as well.

Bow Null

At close to midnight, I ascended the ladder to the control room to prepare to take over the watch. I talked to the team in the sonar and the radio room. I met with the quartermaster, the diving officer, and the chief of the watch. Finally, I read through the ship's logs. Everything was stable for the watch relief. The last thing I reviewed were the captain's night orders. We were to remain submerged and quietly head on a northeasterly course and keep all maritime traffic well outside two nautical miles. We had departed the major shipping lanes and didn't expect any traffic tonight. It was going to be a routine and quiet midwatch… at least I thought.

I was qualified for both engineering officer of the watch (the officer in charge of the engine room with a critical reactor) and officer of the deck (the officer in charge of the ship underway). Although I enjoyed my watches in the engine room, I preferred being the officer of the deck and loved the challenge of navigating the boat and orchestrating everything on board. There's a lot to manage and every watch was a little different. I loved interacting with the team in the control room and the other sailors in sonar, radio, and engineering. I was still pretty new but was gaining knowledge and experience every day.

There were no sonar contacts when I took over the watch, and I settled into the routine of taking care of the ship's business. We had a list of things to do like maintenance, moving water between tanks, and preparing for the morning drill set. I liked the quiet peace of the boat on the midwatch. Most of the crew was asleep, and the pace of activities was generally slower. I usually turned on the speaker to one of the hull-mounted hydrophones to listen to the ocean's sounds. Another bonus to the midwatch was the smell. The cooks were always baking at night, and the aroma of freshly baked bread from the galley would eventually drift into the control room and give me a little reminder of home.

About halfway through the watch, we picked up a distant sonar contact. It was intermittent and very faint. Sonar believed it was a merchant ship off in the distance. The bearing to the contact didn't change very much throughout the night, and the fire control technician estimated the contact was more than ten nautical miles away and heading away from us. I kept an eye on it but it didn't really concern me. The contact was behaving exactly like all the other merchant ships I had encountered. There was no reason to be alarmed.

A few hours later, things changed quickly. Suddenly, the contact's bearing started to change rapidly, which meant it was close. I was trying to process what I saw when sonar picked up loud engine noises coming from the contact, which they confirmed was a large merchant ship. I didn't need their report because I started hearing the ship's engines over the hydrophone speaker. This ship was close! I quickly maneuvered our boat to ensure the towed equipment would be safe if the ship passed directly overhead. Everyone in control listened in shock as this phantom ship passed.

After several tense minutes, it was over. The ship passed inside of two nautical miles of our position. It wasn't directly overhead but it was way too close. I had violated the captain's night orders and let a merchant ship get close to our position. Unfortunately, I needed to wake the captain and give him the bad news.

After the captain awoke, he came to the bridge. I was upset that I let this happen on my watch. The captain was as well. I was still trying to piece together how I had allowed the ship to get so close to us. As I explained the situation to the captain and showed him the sonar and fire control data, he muttered two words – "bow null" – and walked off.

I was confused. What was a "bow null" and how did I miss this? When I got off watch, I talked to several more experienced officers, trying to understand the situation. When I went through the scenario and told them the two words the captain had said, they all laughed. They knew what happened. One of them said to me, "The captain's right. You had a bow null. You've got to get that figured out early, or you'll get run over."

He explained that some of the newer and larger merchant ships were now being built with oversized bulbous bows to increase speed, range, fuel efficiency, and stability. These enormous ship bows hid the engine noises if the ship was pointing directly towards you. In other words, it was impossible to hear these large ships if they were on a direct collision course. They appeared like a distant ship heading away. I had encountered a rare situation of a new merchant ship with a bulbous bow heading directly towards us, creating this bow null effect. He then told me how to address the problem in the future. It was a simple technique to make a significant course change to unmask the bow null. The trick was taking action early in the encounter. Once again, I learned a valuable lesson of how early action can prevent a problem from growing.

There is a universal truth about problems and fires. The longer it takes to attack them, the larger they get. In business, almost every significant issue that gets to senior management was once a smaller problem that could have been resolved in the early stages. That's one reason I believe in having a robust set of key performance indicators (KPIs) to measure the business's performance in real time. Negative trends in price, product mix, customer satisfaction, safety, quality, or on-time delivery will alert the management team. And they can take action before the problems get out of control.

THE BUSINESS WORLD: GREAT APOLOGY TOUR

The multinational company I was working for decided to make an organizational change. At this point in my career I was running several factories. Now, in addition to my current responsibilities, I was being assigned another business. This one was struggling with profitability. I was somewhat familiar with the products and the people in this business, and I thought I understood the problems. But all that changed after my first visit.

There were severe issues in the financial reports. I couldn't believe how much they were spending on warranty and customer concessions. My concern grew as I spoke to all the key managers as I usually do when I take over a new business. I asked three questions of each manager: *What's going well? What's going wrong? And, if you were in my shoes, what would you do first?* In these meetings, there was a consensus. The business had a problem with one of its product lines, and we needed to fix it.

The problematic product line had come into the company through an acquisition. Since the acquired company was small, their product testing was not up to our standards. The previous company never completed any accelerated life testing, which would have revealed a design flaw – the product used a component rated for indoor use in an outdoor environment. After several years exposed to heat, humidity, and moisture, that part would corrode and eventually stop working.

What bothered me most was that this was a known problem that was left to linger. Management knew there was an issue, but all the solutions were difficult and expensive to execute. Instead of making the tough call, they ignored the problem and hoped it would go away. The result was a growing list of angry customers and no long-term plan to fix the problem. This product-quality issue was the submarine equivalent of a fire raging out of control. It grew into a major crisis because the situation wasn't addressed in the early stages.

To fix the product now would require a significant engineering redesign. In addition to the quality problems, the product line was missing many key features and configurations that were available from the competition. Making adjustments would take an unplanned and significant multi-year, multimillion-dollar effort. There was also a consensus that, even with the redesign, the product would continue to have low margins. To make it worse, I also discovered there was new technology coming that would likely make this product line obsolete in the next five to eight years.

It seemed like we were stuck. We couldn't move forward, and we couldn't change the past. So I made the only decision I could make: I killed the product line.

With little hope for a successful redesign, I decided to exit this product immediately. We would fill all open orders and stop taking new ones in just 30 days. It was the nuclear option; and our customers, sales force, and suppliers weren't going to be happy. To minimize the impact on customers, I planned to extend the warranty for the entire installed base. We were exiting this business, but I wanted to let them know we would still support our product.

The final action I had to take was the most difficult. We had a dozen customers with significant field quality problems, so I decided to visit each one and work out a plan to satisfy their concerns. The visits would let customers know how we would support them going forward. They would also help us understand our financial exposure. I called it "The Great Apology Tour." Only, unlike a rock band tour, it wasn't much fun.

I had to sit face-to-face with the customers who had purchased this product over the past eight years and explain why we were exiting the business. I also had to develop a plan to fix the problematic units at each site. The one question I received the most was, "How did you let this happen?" That question was a tough one. How does a major corporation sell a product with a design flaw? How does management allow a minor problem to go unaddressed until it becomes a crisis? The answer was simple: We didn't run to the fire; we ran away.

Missing Binoculars

We had successfully exited the Cumberland Sound, and we were making our way out to the Atlantic Ocean. The order went out to secure the maneuvering watch, a special watch designed for near-shore operations. The plan was to traverse on the surface for eight hours, then submerge and head north. As the lookouts headed down from the bridge, they turned in their binoculars to the quartermaster of the watch. The quartermaster of the watch is the sailor who assists the officer of the deck and the navigator with navigation duties. He is responsible for all navigation operations and equipment. Our departure on this patrol was proceeding according to plan.

I stood the first watch as officer of the deck on the bridge as we headed out to sea. It was summer, the waters were calm, and the sky was full of stars. It was a perfect night to be on the surface, and I enjoyed every minute of the solitude and fresh air. At the end of my watch, my replacement came up to the bridge. I turned over the duty and headed down for dinner. I knew it would be a long time until I saw the sky again. That was the life of a submariner.

A few hours later, the captain summoned us to control. There was a problem. As the current watch was preparing the boat to submerge, one pair of binoculars was discovered missing. It was issued for the maneuvering watch and never returned. *No big deal*, I thought. *I'm sure they'll turn up*. But it was a big deal to our captain. He wanted those binoculars found. He called for everyone who had stood watch that day to search the entire ship for the missing binoculars. No one was going to have any time off until we found them.

I thought it was crazy. We had all been up for more than 20 hours, and we were exhausted. It had been a long day getting the boat ready for sea and making our way out of the tight channel. I couldn't understand why he was making such a big deal about this one set of binoculars. We had a bunch of them on board, and one missing pair wasn't going to make a difference. But since he was the boss, we searched the entire boat.

I helped search the bridge and free-flood areas of the conning tower. It was hard to see in the dark, and I used my Maglite to search every level. I was frustrated, just like the rest of the crew. It seemed futile, and I thought we would never find them. The crew was grumbling and complaining. But after several hours, we found the binoculars. Somehow, they had ended up wedged in the back of the conning tower in an area that would be underwater once we were submerged. I didn't care how they got there; I was just happy to be done with this wild goose chase. I didn't understand why this was such a big deal and thought the captain was overreacting; I was about to learn an important lesson.

The captain called everyone to control to talk about the binoculars. He asked us if we understood why this was such an important issue, why it was mission-critical that we find those missing binoculars. Most of us kept our heads down because we didn't know. He explained that as soon as he learned they were missing, he knew our mission was at risk. He was worried about a solid object sitting unsecured in the superstructure of the boat. Once submerged, the object could create a rattle or a transient noise that could give away our position to the Soviets. We had to find the binoculars before we dove. The captain knew this was a small problem that could magnify and fully compromise our strategic mission. He ran to the fire and demonstrated to the crew the importance of leading from the front. It was a lesson I never forgot.

In any organization, problems appear which could have devastating effects. Like the binoculars, these problems are often small and remain hidden. There is pressure from the group to ignore these problems and hope for the best. It's easy to rationalize them away. But leading from the front means having the wisdom to recognize which problems could grow and, like our captain, doing whatever it takes to solve the problem. Often, people in the organization will think you're crazy and won't understand your persistence. They will fail to see the situation for what it is. You can help your team by sharing the reasons for your concerns.

There are also some problems only the leader can see. Because you have a broader view of the organization, you can see things your team can't. You might see a significant problem developing with a strategic customer or a change in the competitive landscape requiring a new strategy. Like RadioShack, you might sense a considerable market shift or a new technology introduction that would threaten your business. You are the lookout on the bridge watching for hazards. Identifying and attacking these problems with tenacity will set the tone for the rest of the organization.

The Business World: Chasing Gremlins

I had a hard time believing the reports I was receiving from another manufacturing plant in our division. One out of every 100 mechanisms we supplied to them was failing. It didn't make any sense. Every component was built to specifications and assembled precisely into the final product. We operated every mechanism 500 times before shipping it out. There was no way we could be seeing this level of "infant mortality." These mechanisms were designed to operate more than 10,000 times. It just didn't make sense.

The mechanisms were part of a circuit breaker assembled at the sister plant. We had recently moved this component into our manufacturing operation because the original plant where they were built was shutting down. We had the core competencies to make these mechanisms, so we had carefully moved the production line over the past six months. We had a detailed project plan, and we carried it out with precision. Our production teams carefully manufactured and tested each component. They also assembled each mechanism with the same processes and procedures that came from the original plant. I was having a hard time believing what I was hearing.

I called a meeting with my top manufacturing engineers to understand why we were experiencing these failures. Like me, they were all having a hard time understanding the reports coming from the other plant. The failures were intermittent, and the failure mode varied on each mechanism. It was like there were gremlins in our product. The consensus from my team was that there must be something wrong at the other plant. Everything we were doing was correct. The 500 operations we conducted proved there was nothing wrong with the units. My team also reminded me that the other plant had accused us of product failures in the past, which turned out not to be our issue.

While it wasn't clear what was causing these failures, I agreed to send a replacement unit to the other plant anytime there was an issue. Current production levels meant I would supply one extra mechanism every month. Everyone seemed to be happy with this arrangement – everybody except me. Maybe it was just my instincts, and perhaps it was the lessons I learned from the Navy, but I just couldn't let it go. I couldn't understand how we could be having intermittent failures like this, especially with our careful efforts to make the parts. These gremlins were like small, smoldering fires to me and I couldn't ignore them; I had to run toward them.

I decided to talk to some of the engineers at the original manufacturing location. I wanted to understand if they had ever seen intermittent early failures like this. Maybe this was just a design issue. I was surprised to learn that this was confusing to them as well. They had never experienced any failures like this. Something had changed since we moved production into our facility, so I decided to take a closer look at the failed units. We had five failed mechanisms in our quality hold area. I asked our engineers to take them apart and look for any potential failure mode. Despite our careful efforts, I had to assume that we were doing something wrong.

Each mechanism contained more than 80 parts, most of them manufactured on our production lines. Some of the parts were zinc-plated, and some were painted. Others were heat-treated to make them harder and more durable. When the engineers dissected the units, they discovered something they didn't expect. A few of the heat-treated parts were slightly deformed, which they saw under a magnifying glass. Something was wrong with these parts. After testing their hardness, the engineers discovered the problem: The failed components had not been heat-treated after all. For some reason, these parts made it to the assembly station without going through the heat-treatment process. They were too soft, and this was causing the failures.

We discovered that our operators, by mistake, would occasionally move parts to the assembly line that had not been heat-treated. We also learned there was no easy way to catch this on the line. It was hard to visually tell the difference between a part that had been heat-treated and one that hadn't. The heat-treated part was slightly darker, but it was nearly impossible for a production worker on the assembly line to recognize this. We were able to fix this problem by simply adding a new step to the heat-treating process. We placed a silver-painted dot on every part coming out of the heat-treat furnaces. We trained the operators on the line to look for the silver dot before using the part. It was a simple fix.

From that point on the failures stopped. We slayed the gremlins. More importantly, we developed a process for identifying heat-treated parts that we could use on all our other product lines. When I considered other unexplained failures I'd heard about over the years, I wondered how many could have been avoided by this simple fix. I wondered how many times we ignored the warning signs and didn't search for a root cause, or how many times we didn't run to the fire.

The Bottom Line

Key Points

- Run towards problems, not away from them.
- Lead from the front.
- Attack problems while they are still small.
- Celebrate those who run to the fire.
- Build a smooth-running business where firefighting is rare.

Tweetable Quotes

Tweet the following quotes with these hashtags: #allinthesameboat #runtothefire

"Leading from the front means having the wisdom to recognize which problems could grow and doing whatever it takes to solve the problem."

"Like a lookout on the bridge of a ship, leaders see hazards before the rest of their team."

"There is a universal truth about problems and fires: The longer it takes to attack them, the larger they get."

"Almost every significant issue an organization faces was once a smaller problem that could have been resolved easily in the early stages."

"It's the leader's job to build a stable, smooth-running business."

"Successful leaders empower employees and give them the tools and authority to resolve issues before they escalate."

Questions to Ponder

1. Can you think of a major issue in your organization that was once a smaller problem that could have been resolved in the early stages?

2. What are you doing to create and foster a problem-solving culture?

3. Name one problem facing your organization that you are running away from and not running towards.

4. What can you do to reverse course?

Chapter 2. Earn Your Oxygen

Life is simple. You're either qualified or you're not. – Anonymous submariner

Dolphin Pinning

It was a beautiful spring morning in southeast Georgia, and the Trident Nuclear Submarine Refit Facility in Kings Bay was dressed up for the occasion. So was the *USS Tennessee*, which was sitting proudly on display. The slight breeze blowing through the building caused the patriotic buntings and banners to shimmer and wave in the light. Families, dressed in their Sunday best, murmured in excitement for what was about to happen. The admirals and generals were all on hand as well, their ribbons and medals proudly on display. They were trying to look stoic, but they also knew this day was special. It was only a year after Operation Desert Storm. There was still a sense of proud patriotism in the country.

The officers and crew of the *Tennessee* stood at attention on the deck of the home they had lived in for the past three months. Proudly clad in their dress white uniforms, they stood in stark contrast to the $2 billion warship's black steel hull. Military music echoed through the facility as the Navy band continued to play to the assembled crowd. As I stood at attention and took in the scene, I was filled with emotions.

This event was historically significant. It wasn't just that the *Tennessee* had returned from another successful deployment; this ceremony represented a significant milestone in the Cold War. The *USS Tennessee* had just completed the nation's 3,000th strategic deterrent patrol. That meant that since the *USS George Washington* first set sail from Charleston, South Carolina, in November of 1960, U.S. submarines had patrolled the ocean 3,000 times. For 32 years sailors had left their families to quietly watch over the nation from the ocean's depths.

At the time, I didn't realize that this ceremony was also the first major celebration of the end of the Cold War. The USSR officially dissolved, breaking up into 15 separate nations, just four short months earlier. The prolonged standoff was over, and the gathered dignitaries understood the significance of this day. I was now part of the long line of submariners who kept the country safe during this dark time in our history.

It had been a long deployment and, like the rest of the crew, I was happy to be home. But unlike most of them, I was feeling something else that day: pride. This event also marked an important day in my naval career. I had been chasing a dream for seven years, and I was about to achieve it.

The entire chain of command, from my commanding officer to

General Colin Powell, the chairman of the Joint Chiefs of Staff, was on hand for the ceremony. It was a big deal. The Chief of Naval Operations, Admiral Frank Kelso, had the honor of introducing General Powell, who delivered the keynote speech. I knew Admiral Kelso was a submariner who, like me, had spent months at sea on patrol, but General Powell was Army. I wondered what he thought about submariners like us.

General Powell spoke glowingly about the *Tennessee*, her "magnificent crew," and the significance of this particular patrol, but his comments about the Cold War submarine sailor hit home. The following is a short excerpt from his speech that day:

> *No one has done more to prevent conflict. No one has made a greater sacrifice for the cause of peace than you, America's proud missile submarine family. You stand tall among all our heroes of the Cold War. To a soldier like me, sailors are different. Wonderfully different. I never cease to be awed by the extraordinary dedication and devotion to duty shown by you who go down to the sea in ships in defense of your country. Routinely, for months on end, the sailor endures a brand of hardship that the rest of us in uniform seldom face – separation, loneliness, deprivation, confinement. We owe a debt*

> *of gratitude to our sailors and to their families. And a special debt is owed to you who wear the dolphins so proudly on your chests.*

General Powell seemed to have a deep understanding of the unique life of the submariner. His words visibly moved the crowd. I remained at attention and listened respectfully to every word, but when he talked about sailors proudly wearing dolphins, I smiled. I smiled because today was the day I would finally get mine. Today was the day I would become qualified.

Submarine dolphins are a Navy insignia worn on the uniform to signify an officer or enlisted sailor is qualified in submarine warfare. The officer dolphins are gold, and the enlisted dolphins are silver. It marks the end of an intensive, year-long effort to prove your proficiency in every submarine system, procedure, casualty response, tactical action, and watch station. New officers and sailors reporting to a boat get a blank qualification card, also known as a "qual card." To get qualified, you must obtain hundreds of signatures from experienced officers and sailors, proving your knowledge and skills in every area of submarine operations. When you see someone wearing dolphins, you know they have been through a grueling experience. They have proven themselves worthy of wearing the badge.

At the end of the ceremony, the admirals, generals, and VIPs began to depart. The band stopped playing. The refit facility quietly echoed with sounds of wives, children, and parents happily welcoming their sailors home. My family met me topside for the small dolphin pinning event that was about to take place. I was rail-thin, and my uniform appeared to be two sizes too big. I also looked like I hadn't slept in weeks. The truth was, I hadn't. Being unqualified on a submarine is an uncomfortable place to be. I had just spent the past year trying to prove I had what it took to be called a submariner. Getting qualified and earning my dolphins was a dream that took seven long years to achieve.

During the pinning event, I was surrounded by family as my wife pinned on my dolphins for the first time. We had been married only five months, three of which I had been at sea. It was an emotional moment. I looked down at the shiny gold insignia on my chest, and I couldn't believe it. It was the most incredible feeling, one that I will never forget. I had achieved my goals, proved my mettle, and I was now a qualified submariner. I looked around the refit facility, and a memory came rushing back from a year earlier. This building was the exact place where I first saw the *USS Tennessee* as an ensign fresh out of submarine school. Back then I was young, inexperienced, and overwhelmed. Now I was a little older and wiser and, more importantly, I was qualified.

On a submarine and in business, the more skills you know, the more valuable you are. Being qualified means that others can depend on you to do your job. In the Navy, this was a life-or-death situation. You literally relied on the competency of your shipmates to keep you alive. In business, there isn't the same pressure. However, organizations that place a high emphasis on training and learning will outperform their rivals which is why it's in everyone's best interest to train new employees.

The Navy's approach to qualification is unique, and companies can learn valuable lessons by observing these key principles. The organization's overall capability will be further enhanced when every employee has been trained and knows what to do.

NUB Life

It was Saturday night on my second patrol, and I headed up to the wardroom for supper. Saturday night was always special at sea because it was pizza night. It was time to shake up the regular meal rotation and enjoy some tastes of home. The crew always cherished pizza night. It meant another week had passed, and we were one week closer to home. I loved the pizza night tradition, although if I'm honest, the pizza was never all that good. Still, it was nice to kick back and enjoy a casual meal with my shipmates.

For the officers, Saturday night almost always included a movie and a poker game as well. It was a chance to relax and burn off some steam after a long week. Everyone enjoyed Saturday nights on patrol. That is, of course, if you were qualified. And at this point, I wasn't. It takes about a year to complete the submarine qualification process once you get to the fleet, and I was almost finished. There is no doubt I was jealous of the other officers who were.

When the meal was over, I quietly listened as the officers with dolphins on their uniforms debated which movie they would watch. I listened enviously to their discussion. There were great movies on board, and I would have loved the chance to escape submarine life for a few hours. But that wasn't going to happen. Not now.

"What are you looking at, NUB? Go get some signatures on your qual card if you want to catch a flick." There it was. I wasn't qualified, and they let me know it. I wasn't yet a valuable part of the crew. I was a NUB, a "Non-Useful Body." It's a colorful term used on a submarine to denote a new officer or sailor recently out of school and not yet qualified. It kept the pressure on unqualified crew members to work hard on their qualifications. On a submarine, life was simple; you were either qualified, or you weren't. Without dolphins, I was just a NUB. I wasn't yet carrying my load, which meant I was taking food and oxygen from other qualified crew members who had earned it. To the qualified submariner, a NUB is an annoyance at best and a liability at worst. It wasn't much fun being one.

The truth is, the peer pressure on the boat worked. It was effective on me and everyone else who had ever been in my shoes. We all wanted to belong. We all wanted to carry our load, and we certainly didn't want to be a liability. So despite being tired, annoyed, and sometimes overwhelmed with the process, we trudged on. We worked hard to finish our qualifications. We worked hard to join the ranks of the qualified.

With my notebook, a cup of black coffee, and my dog-eared qual card, I headed down to the torpedo room to work on my torpedo system qualifications. I knew the guys on this watch would be a little more helpful than the guys on the last watch. Part of the challenge of the qualification process is knowing where to go to get signatures. Some sailors were quick to help the new guys. They were natural teachers, and they loved seeing new guys learn essential concepts.

Other guys were tough, and they sent you away if you didn't know the answers to their demanding and often obscure questions. Getting their signatures was always more challenging, but you ended up learning so much more. I didn't mind the tough guys. What I couldn't stand were the guys who just wanted to harass you. They seemed to take pure joy in giving NUBs a hard time. These were the sailors who sent you around the boat looking for imaginary objects like relative-bearing grease, a bucket of steam, or water slugs. I tried to avoid them at all costs.

That night I spent close to six hours in the torpedo room. I got all the signatures needed to complete my torpedo systems qualification. The sailors there were quick to teach me everything I needed to know. They showed me the location of critical valves, how the torpedo display worked, and reviewed all the various torpedo casualties. It was a long night, but while the other officers watched movies and played cards, I moved one step closer to getting qualified. All in all, it was a good night.

The Navy taught me valuable lessons about getting qualified. I learned how uncomfortable it was to be unqualified and how it made you feel like an outcast, not yet part of the family. I felt the shame of not being able to stand watch and pull my own weight. But I also saw how that pressure drove me to work hard to get qualified, to gain the knowledge and experience to become an effective submariner. These lessons stayed with me throughout my business career.

The Business World: Skill Stacking

It was my first week as quality manager, and I was already being tested. I was hosting a team of auditors from several electric utilities who were examining our quality systems for compliance with the nuclear power quality assurance standards. The manufacturing plant where I worked supplied critical components to civilian nuclear power plants. I had been out of the Navy for just two years, but I felt like I was back on the boat in the middle of an Operational Reactor Safeguard Examination (ORSE). I had been tested so many times in the Navy this seemed normal. What wasn't normal was how quickly I moved into this role.

When I first got out of the Navy and started working for a multinational engineering company, I was hired as an associate design engineer. It was the lowest position for an engineer at the company. For me, it felt like being an ensign. I was new and inexperienced. I had that uncomfortable feeling of being a NUB all over again, and I hated it. I was determined to get qualified and contribute just like on the boat.

However, I quickly learned that "qualifying" in corporate America is a lot different from the Navy. Nobody hands you a qual card and shows you the way. You're pretty much on your own. During my first few weeks I didn't even know what to do. Everybody seemed to be busy except me. My boss hadn't assigned me to a project yet. I found myself helping organize and file engineering drawings, and I was beginning to question why the company had even hired me. It wasn't long until I fell back on my experiences in the Navy. I figured the only way to get qualified is to take the initiative, and I decided it was time for me to find a way to learn from the more senior employees as I had in the Navy.

I spoke to the entire department at the next engineering meeting and asked a simple favor. If anyone was going out on the manufacturing floor or working on anything interesting, get me. Show me what you do and teach me what goes on here. I acknowledged that I needed their help getting up to speed, and that simple request changed everything. I discovered that everyone was willing to share what they knew. I just had to ask. They saw I was eager to learn and wanted to contribute, so they were happy to help.

For months on end I was like a puppy, following the senior

engineers around and learning about the business. I asked questions, took notes, studied engineering standards, spent time on the shop floor, and took everything in. I also had to learn to use the AutoCAD software to create engineering drawings, which was entirely new to me. After about six months I became a contributing member of the engineering team, and my boss began assigning me projects. I could have been content with a career as a design engineer, but it felt like there was more for me to learn. In a way, it was a lot like the boat. I started in engineering but I wanted to do more.

Each month the company had all-employee meetings where management shared what was going on in the business. In almost every meeting they asked for volunteers for various projects happening on site. The first time I heard them ask for volunteers, I laughed to myself. In the Navy, we had a saying for that: "NAVY stands for Never Again Volunteer Yourself." I could see that mindset must have existed in the civilian world too because no one stepped up. No one wanted any extra work. For me, I saw it as an opportunity. If I wanted to learn more about the business, I had to find ways to get involved in areas outside of engineering. And I did that by volunteering for everything.

I became active with the human resource department, helping lead the activities committee and rolling out an employee survey. I got involved with the information technology department to integrate a new enterprise resource planning (ERP) software system into the business. I also became certified as an ISO 9001 internal quality auditor, a nuclear quality assurance auditor, and a vendor quality auditor. In my mind, each of these volunteer assignments was like qualifying on a watch station. I figured the more I knew, the more valuable I would be to the company. What I didn't realize at the time is that I was stacking skills.

Skill stacking is the idea that you can combine several ordinary skills to create a combination of abilities to become extremely valuable. Scott Adams, the *Dilbert* comic strip creator, actually coined the phrase "talent stack" to describe this concept. In his book, *How to Fail at Almost Everything and Still Win Big*, Adams says, "Every skill you acquire doubles your odds of success." The extra work I was doing was creating a valuable skill stack, and it got the attention of upper management.

Just two short years out of the Navy, the division vice president offered me the quality manager position. They promoted the previous manager and needed someone with engineering knowledge, leadership experience, and a strong understanding of nuclear quality assurance procedures. There was no one else in the business who met those criteria. My skill stack made me a perfect match for the job. With very little guidance and support, I was able to get qualified and move into a leadership position.

In my first real action as the quality manager, I demonstrated to the auditors that our company complied with the nuclear power quality assurance standards. We passed the audit with no findings and maintained all our certifications. For the next two years I successfully served as quality manager while continuing to learn about the business and the industry. I kept building my skill stack until, at just 32 years old, my boss selected me to become a plant manager.

The qualification process in the submarine Navy had prepared me well for corporate life. The uncomfortable feeling of being unqualified drove me to find ways to gain knowledge, and I learned from more experienced employees just like I did back on the *Tennessee*. By chance, I also discovered the value of skill stacking, becoming more valuable to the company as I acquired knowledge and experience. My unique stack of skills made me the perfect candidate for a promotion that started me on my leadership journey in the corporate world. I learned that getting qualified wasn't just something for military life.

Let Them Fail

I cleared the baffles and looked for any contacts in my wake. I was preparing the *Tennessee* to go to periscope depth. Regardless of how many times I had done this, taking the ship to periscope depth was always tricky. We were vulnerable from the time we left the comfort of deeper depths until the periscope broke the surface. There are many things in the ocean that don't make noise. These dangers – such as sailboats, old shipping containers, logs, and debris – would cause significant damage to our sub if we hit them. I had already learned my lesson about bow nulls, so I was especially careful to make sure conditions were clear.

Once we were ready and I was confident there were no ships in the area, I called the captain. I gave him a full briefing and requested permission to take the boat to periscope depth. Once I received approval, I started the procedure I had done a hundred times before.

I was on my fifth patrol, and at this point I was a seasoned officer who had stood countless watches as officer of the deck. I was now a fully qualified lieutenant and had stood so many watches as officer of the deck that I had become an expert. Instead of chasing down signatures on my qual card, I was now the guy the NUBs came looking for to prove their knowledge. Today I was training a NUB as a junior officer of the deck, and he was about to have a bad day.

As I raised the #1 periscope, I reviewed the plan in my head: Take the ship to periscope depth and make sure the conditions were clear. Then, bring the boat safely down to 130 feet and turn over the watch to my trainee. The plan was for him to make an ascent to periscope depth during a simulated ship casualty of my choosing. I wanted to test his mettle today and see how quickly he could get the boat to periscope depth in the event of a fire. I also wanted to assess how well he could operate the periscope without hydraulic assistance. I was testing both his mental and physical toughness. I hoped he was ready.

I looked through the periscope and dialed the optics straight up so that I could keep an eye out for any dangers. I rotated the scope to look for shapes and shadows, anything that could be a threat to the boat. I began my search, keeping a careful watch of everything around us. The scope spun freely using the hydraulic assist, and I quickly got into a good pace. Once I was comfortable with the conditions, I gave the order to go to periscope depth.

As the ship ascended, the control room went utterly silent except for the diving officer calling out the depths. Everyone was listening to me. With my periscope sweeps, I was the eyes of the ship, and what I said in the next ten minutes would be critical. Everyone listened for me to say one phrase, "no close contacts." If I said anything else, they would abort the attempt and safely bring the ship to deeper depths. The pitch-black ocean lightened as we ascended, and I began to see the blue-green water shimmering in the sunlight. Everything went as planned, and the scope broke the surface. The water cleared the optics, and I made two full sweeps looking for any ships or debris on the surface. Everything was clear, so I shouted, "no close contacts."

We stayed at periscope depth for about 20 minutes while my junior officer of the deck operated the scope. I walked him through all of the features and functions. He would need the ability to use the periscope in the dark and without taking his eyes off the optics. Everything would need to be done entirely by touch. Once I completed the training session, we returned to 130 feet to prepare for the drill. I wasn't sure my trainee was ready, but it was his turn to prove himself.

The captain came into control for the drill set. Like me, he wanted to see if this young officer was progressing in his training. The junior officer of the deck was young and fresh out of submarine school. He was an ensign and a NUB. He was technically smart and seemed to learn quickly, but he was small in stature. This drill would require physical strength. Rotating the periscope dozens of times without hydraulics was difficult, even for a big guy. I was worried he would struggle.

The young ensign took over as officer of the deck as we prepared to start the drill. Even though he had the watch, he was still under my supervision. Ultimately, I was responsible for the ship and kept a close eye on everything he did. When the drill started, everything happened fast. Alarms were buzzing, and casualty reports were coming into control as the damage control team rushed in to set up their command post. The simulated fire quickly knocked out lighting, air conditioning, and some of the hydraulic systems. The young NUB did his best to direct the casualty actions as he prepared the boat to go back to periscope depth. He knew he needed to get to the surface quickly to ventilate the smoke from the simulated fire.

With the air conditioning out of commission, the conditions in control quickly became stale, and you could feel the temperature rising. The young officer assessed the contact situation and requested permission to go to periscope depth. Then things got ugly.

As he mounted the scope and gave the order to go to periscope depth, I turned off the hydraulic assist to simulate a loss of hydraulics. Like driving a car without power steering, it would take all his strength. As I expected, he struggled. He rotated the scope slowly, using all his strength. He used his legs to give him leverage but the scope barely moved. It wasn't going fast enough to do a proper search, and I was beginning to worry. I also noticed he was sweating profusely in the warm, stale air in control, and his glasses kept fogging up. I didn't think this was safe at all.

After five minutes of watching this epic struggle, I couldn't take it anymore. I was worried about the safety of the boat. We were at a vulnerable depth, and the periscope sweeps were inadequate. There was no way he could identify threats, and I was still responsible for the boat on this watch. So I did what I thought was right – I began to help him rotate the periscope. That was a big mistake.

The captain stopped me in my tracks. He shouted, "Let him do it!" I tried to argue but the captain looked me right in the eye and spoke very clearly and sternly: "Let him do it." So I backed off. The captain was ultimately in charge, and he knew what he was doing. I watched in disbelief as the captain allowed the young officer to continue to struggle to periscope depth. When the optics cleared, he conducted two slow sweeps and reported "no close contacts." We were in the clear.

After the drill's conclusion, I took back the watch, and the junior officer of the deck and captain left control. I breathed a sigh of relief. The whole training session had been stressful, and I just wanted this watch to be over. I felt I had done the right thing to help the young officer but was trying to understand why the captain had been so angry with me.

While lying in my rack that night, I thought about the events of the day. I tried to rationalize why my actions were correct and why the captain was wrong. I tried to understand the captain's motives. I felt like I had failed. Then it hit me; I had failed.

I realized that, as I was observing the ensign, the captain was watching me. He was seeing how good I was at training new officers. He was evaluating me. I also realized that he was ultimately responsible for the ship's safety and was fully confident the ship was safe. I had overreacted and didn't let the new officer fail. I didn't let him feel the full effects of failure and the benefits of learning what he would ultimately gain from that.

Failure is an essential aspect of training on a submarine. Under controlled conditions, we let people fail. It is a powerful teaching tool. Nobody wants to fail, so failure creates a deep emotional response. It forces us to question what we did wrong and how to get better. Ultimately, my failure in training this new officer helped me become a better instructor. His failure on the scope helped him become a better officer of the deck. We both grew because of this event.

In business, most companies don't take the time to allow employees to experience controlled failure. They are too busy. They need to get the orders out, land that big account, and make the numbers. They barely have time to train people, and they definitely don't have time for failure. Most companies give challenging assignments to senior people to make sure things go right. They assign low-risk projects to new people so they don't screw up. Because of this, they miss out on the powerful lessons that come from failure.

The Navy taught me the importance of failure. I have tried to use this principle to develop both new and high-potential employees. One technique I have successfully used in the business world is stretch assignments. Stretch assignments are a great way to develop and evaluate new talent. I've learned that if you give an employee a challenging task and an opportunity to fail in controlled conditions, you can discover a lot about that person. Some employees will use these experiences to learn and get better; others will fold under pressure. As a leader, this is powerful information. Knowing how people respond to failure will help you build the best team possible.

A Qualified Team

We had been at battle stations torpedo for more than an hour. There was a Soviet submarine trailing us, and we were doing our best to get into a better tactical position. During battle stations, my job was to act as the geographic plot operator, also known as the "geoplot" operator. The geoplot was a large table with a blank sheet of paper on it. A white dot under the table represented our position and moved as we moved. As information about our adversaries came in, I would plot them with colored pencils onto the paper. Over time, a clear picture of our tactical situation would emerge. In the high-tech world of nuclear submarine operations, this simple, low-tech process was one of the most valuable tools we used in battle.

During battle stations, the geoplot operator was usually a seasoned officer who could take volumes of data and determine an accurate tactical picture. It was part art, part science, and I was good at it. It was so crucial during battle stations that the captain would stand next to me as I determined what each threat was doing. The geoplot represented the big picture, and it helped the captain decide what to do next. Often I would be tracking multiple surface ships and a submarine at the same time. It was tedious and challenging work but I loved it. Today I was focusing on one Soviet boat.

Our battle stations team was deeply experienced and acutely familiar with each other. We had been together for several years in the tight confines of the *Tennessee*. All of us were immensely capable in our individual roles, and together we were an unbeatable team. We were so familiar with each other that we could signal what we wanted just by a look or voice tone. For example, when I first took over the geoplot responsibilities, the captain taught me a simple thumb rule. He said that the MK48 torpedo was so capable that I didn't need to know precisely where the target was for him to make a good shot. He said that as long as I could put my hand on the geoplot and know the target was somewhere under my hand, we could hit it. Many times, in the simulator, he would look at me and hold out his hand. I always knew what he was asking. He wanted to know if I had the target position narrowed down to the size of my hand. It was the last piece of information he needed before he took the shot.

Today I was struggling to figure out what this Soviet boat was doing. We had intermittent contact, and it appeared as though the sub had changed course several times. I recommended we maneuver to determine what the target was doing. Listening to a contact from a different angle helped us triangulate the position and determine the range. When we steadied on the new course, we picked up the Soviet boat again. It was precisely where I thought he would be. After a few calculations, I had a solution. I knew exactly what this other submarine was doing. I put my hand on the geoplot over the Soviet boat's position and smiled confidently. The captain saw it. He knew I had him.

"Fire One!" the captain commanded as we all heard the familiar sound of an MK48 torpedo leaving the boat. The torpedo ran hot, straight, and normal. The Soviet boat reacted by increasing speed and maneuvering away from the incoming torpedo. But it was too late as we scored a direct hit. My captain looked over at me and smiled. Once again, we took out another Soviet boat in the simulator. The base training officers had done their best to give us problematic scenarios to try to confuse us, but we were too good as a team. We rarely missed a shot.

There is something special about being a part of a qualified team. When you have an experienced leader and are surrounded by knowledgeable and proficient peers, you feel unbeatable. In a competent team, there is positive pressure to improve your skills. No one wants to let the team down. There is also zero tolerance for infighting or backstabbing. Qualified teams know that the enemy is outside the four walls, or in our case, outside the steel hull. All of the team's energy focuses on defeating the opponent, not each other.

Another unique aspect of the crew of a submarine is that there is no shortcut to advancement. To be promoted or get qualified on a watch station, you had to put in your time. You had to do the hard work and gain the experience. This meant you always knew your peers were just as skilled and qualified as you were. They had put in their time, and they were proficient. There was mutual respect in the team.

We held our leaders in high regard as well. We knew they had walked the same walk as us and had done everything we had to do and more. Every ship's captain was once a young, inexperienced ensign. Every submarine leader started from the bottom and earned his right to take on more responsibility. Our leaders were all competent and skilled in the art of submarine warfare. We had a deep respect for our chain of command. Through training and development, you can replicate this in any organization as well.

The Business World: Startup Team

As CEO of the small manufacturing startup company I co-founded, I was working the back end of one of our production lines. When I helped out on the shop floor, this was the job I liked the most. I was packing the completed products as they came off the line. That meant I was the last person to touch the product before our customers opened it. My job was to complete the final quality check, ensure everything was perfect, and then seal the boxes. I enjoyed working at this station because I felt a connection with our customers. Plus, it gave me a full view of the factory. I could see all my employees, which only totaled nine people at this time.

Today was an important day. We were running both our production lines. We were busy filling orders from several large customers. I knew these customers were testing us. They liked our product and pricing, but they were probably concerned about whether our small company could keep up with their demand. Today was the first day we had ever operated both production lines simultaneously, and everything was running smoothly. We had one employee handling all the customer communications, order entry, and shipping logistics in the office while everyone else was working on the production lines. As I looked around, I smiled. This group of people was an exceptional team.

We hadn't yet hired any production workers. Everyone on the line was a salaried employee, but no one complained. They were all as excited as I was to see both production lines running at the same time. They knew how vital these orders were, and they were willing to do what it took to satisfy these customers. There was a sense of pride that day. Every member of this small team had worked for two solid years to see this day, and, like me, they were taking it all in.

When we first saw the building that would be our factory one day, we were all filled with doubt. It seemed there was no way this decrepit structure could ever be a world-class manufacturing plant. It was an old steel building built in the 1970s. It was dark, dirty, and unheated. As we walked around, we saw broken windows, busted pipes, and rusted equipment. We had to step over the tangled wires that were strewn haphazardly throughout the poorly lit space. It looked like a war zone, and there was a strong smell that permeated everything. It was the fragrant smell of dried tobacco leaves. It created a warm, comforting, nostalgic, familiar, almost intoxicating feeling in the space. This old building was on the campus of a tobacco processing company that had since moved away. Some of the buildings on the property were built in the 1920s. It was a throwback to a different time in America, and we weren't sure if we could ever bring it back to life.

Our team was small but highly capable. Each member had at least a decade of industry experience, and most had advanced technical degrees. Everyone had left the relative comfort of large companies to build something from the ground up. We all shared the common vision of creating a great company. In a way, we were rebels. We were rebelling from corporate life and the soul-crushing, mind-numbing rules and norms that went along with it. We were escaping the world of conference calls and cubicles to make our own dent in the universe.

While I knew each team member was highly qualified and had a proven track record of success, I also discovered something I didn't know. This team had a unique and special capability, something I didn't necessarily intend to build. I found the individuals on our team had a perfect set of complementary skills. With just nine employees, we had every talent we needed to accomplish our objective.

In a way, we were like a SEAL team. In the Navy, SEAL teams use the concept of complementary skill sets. There are specialists like medics, snipers, jumpmasters, divemasters, linguists, and explosives experts. Even though there are overlapping skills, experts are heavily relied on by the team for success in specific areas of the mission. We had used this same concept in our team as well.

We relied heavily on our experts as we transitioned through the various phases of building the business from the ground up. We always seemed to have someone who was an expert and knew how to lead the project when we reached various stages. With only nine people, we had the capability of a team ten times our size. Like a SEAL team, we had the capability of a small army.

On a submarine and in business, the more skills you know, the more valuable you are. What I learned in the Navy was reinforced during this business startup. It proved once again that a team of trained, qualified employees is hard to beat. Our small company was highly capable. We completed these critical orders and continued to gain more and more business. We went on to compete against multinational corporations and took market share. Customers noted our performance and awarded us with ever-increasing orders. We had successfully built this business from a vision and an old, broken-down tobacco plant into a world-class company. We were all proud of the company we had created.

The Bottom Line

Key Points

- The more skills you know, the more valuable you are.
- Being qualified means others can depend on you to do your job.
- It is in the best interest of the team to train new employees.
- New employees should be given opportunities to gain skills and experience.
- Failure is a powerful teaching tool.
- A team of highly trained employees is hard to beat.

Tweetable Quotes

Tweet the following quotes with these hashtags: #allinthesameboat #earnyouroxygen

"An unqualified employee is an annoyance at best and a liability at worst."

"It should be uncomfortable to be unqualified."

"Organizations that place a high emphasis on training and development will outperform their rivals."

"The goal of every leader should be to create a team of highly qualified individuals."

"Failure is a powerful teaching tool. It creates a deep emotional response, forcing us to question what went wrong."

"When you only give tough assignments to senior people and low-risk projects to junior people, you miss out on the powerful lessons of failure."

"Teams made up of knowledgeable and proficient professionals led by an experienced leader are unbeatable."

"On a qualified team, there is zero tolerance for infighting and backstabbing."

Questions to Ponder

1. What does it mean to be "qualified" in your organization?

2. What processes are in place to give new employees opportunities to gain skills and experience?

3. How are you using "controlled failure" as a teaching tool?

4. Can you think of an example of a highly qualified team that you either worked with or knew about? What made them so special?

Chapter 3. Communicate with Precision

Be precise. A lack of precision is dangerous when the margin of error is small.
– Donald Rumsfeld

Formal over Familiar

Everything I needed for the next three months was unpacked from my seabag and neatly placed in the locker under my rack. *It isn't much*, I thought, *but then again, the Navy will likely provide everything else*. My bunk on this deployment was not in "officer country." As an unqualified ensign on my first patrol, I would be staying in the nine-man enlisted berthing. I had the middle rack on a three-high bunk bed. There were nine of us staying in an area the size of a walk-in closet. Most people would have considered these tight quarters, but having made a short run on a fast-attack sub, I knew this was luxury living for a submariner.

In the last few hours the hatch had been shut, and we were headed out to the North Atlantic. I didn't really think about it because I was still trying to get my bearings. I was taking in all the sights, smells, and sounds around me. Sailors and officers were busy moving about the ship, preparing for the long journey. Everyone seemed to know what to do and where to go. I, on the other hand, was the new guy. I had never been to sea on a ballistic missile submarine. Despite my training, I really didn't know what I was supposed to do. I was just trying to stay out of the way.

I wandered up to the officer's study. This was a small room with bench seats and a table where officers would converge to study, train, meet, or just hang out between watches. I figured someone up there would know I was on board and what I should be doing.

I was in luck. Sitting around the table were most of the lieutenants. These were the "senior" junior officers. They had made several patrols and had completed their submarine qualifications. They were only a few years older than I was, but they appeared as wise sages. This was not their first rodeo or their first patrol. They knew what to do and what to expect. They had been in my shoes only a few years earlier, and, thankfully, they were willing to help me get acclimated.

One of the lieutenants agreed to take me on a tour of the engine room. As my first job on board would be to lead the reactor controls department and qualify as engineering officer of the watch (EOOW), this made sense. I needed to meet the team, understand the engine room's layout, and know the location of essential equipment. I'd be spending a lot of time here on this patrol.

He introduced me to various crew members and showed me

around every level of the engine room. I took it all in. When we got to maneuvering, a cramped space that served as the engine room's operations center, we stopped at a small chain that was clipped in front of the entrance. My guide spoke to the officer in charge, the EOOW: "Request permission to enter maneuvering." The EOOW responded, "Enter maneuvering." My tour guide replied, "Enter maneuvering, aye."

Whoa! What just happened? I thought. These guys were the same rank and were probably good friends. I expected to hear friendly banter between two colleagues, not this formal back-and-forth dialogue. The EOOW saw my bewildered look and explained, "Rule #1, you never enter maneuvering without permission from the EOOW." *Okay,* I thought. He continued, "Rule #2, you better have a good reason to be in here." As I looked around at all the indicator panels, controls, and the three other watchstanders – the throttleman, reactor operator, and electrical operator – I realized this was a serious place. I had just entered the control room of an operating nuclear power plant at sea. It was at that moment I began to understand the importance of formal communications and the purpose of "verbatim repeat-back."

Verbatim repeat-back is a practice used throughout the Navy to ensure orders are executed perfectly. It's a formal means of communication to ensure complex equipment is operated correctly and safely. It requires watchstanders to repeat all commands back to the watch officer word for word. You've probably seen it before in movies and thought it was just Hollywood fiction. There's usually a climactic battle scene in military films where the steely-eyed captain gives an epic command to a young sailor who repeats it back intensely. The real Navy isn't quite that dramatic, but there is truth behind this trope.

The 1995 submarine movie *Crimson Tide* starring Gene Hackman and Denzel Washington did a good job portraying what verbatim repeat-back looks like. When the *USS Alabama* first heads out to sea in the movie, you get a sense of what it sounds like to be on a submarine. The commands are precise and executed flawlessly. The commanding officer and executive officer come down from the bridge and announce that all men are down, and hatches are secured. The officer of the deck then gives the command, "Diving officer, submerge the ship. Make your depth 150 feet." This is repeated back by the diving officer, "Submerge the ship. Make my depth 150 feet. Aye, sir."

This movie demonstrates the simplicity and purpose of verbatim repeat-back. It is a process that confirms perfect alignment between a watchstander and watch officer before the order is executed. An order from the officer of the deck to the diving officer might sound something like this: "Dive, make your depth 450 feet. Do not exceed a three degree down bubble." The diving officer would repeat the command back by saying, "Make my depth 450 feet. Do not exceed a three degree down bubble. Aye, sir."

There are two primary purposes for this particular

communications method: (1) It ensures understanding. The leader is provided an opportunity to check whether the watchstander heard and fully understood the command given. A proper verbatim repeat-back tells the watch officer that the watchstander heard the command and understands what to do. (2) It allows the watchstander to internalize the message. Before repeating the command, the watchstander has a chance to think about the order. If he missed or didn't understand part of the command, he could respond, "Say again, sir" or "Say again more clearly, sir" or even "Say again the last part, sir." Both parties have a chance to make sure the command is clearly understood before it is executed.

There are two secondary purposes as well: (1) Verbatim repeat-back promotes professionalism and a standard way to communicate throughout the ship. Watchstanders spend countless hours together at sea and can become too familiar and informal with each other. Keeping things formal prevents miscommunication and costly mistakes. (2) It also demonstrates calm under pressure. Operating a warship at sea is stressful even without contact with the enemy. Having a standard way to give and receive commands when things are quiet and during the pressure of a casualty provides a level of repetition and comfort. Officers and crew members can focus on giving and carrying out the commands in the moment without emotion or panic.

While I've never had a leadership role in business where I felt the need to implement communications as formal as verbatim repeat-back, I still have learned many lessons from this technique. The first lesson is obvious. I've learned to double-check with my team members to make sure there is a clear understanding of every assignment, giving them opportunities to clarify the request. I also like to follow up early in a project to ensure everything is still understood. There is nothing more frustrating for both parties than an employee completing an important assignment incorrectly because he or she misunderstood the boss. The second and most important lesson is the concept of internalization. This powerful lesson is often missed by most leaders.

Verbatim repeat-back works in a simple but impactful way. In the Navy, watchstanders hear a command, think about how they will carry out that command, then repeat it back to their watch officer. By this simple technique, they internalize the assignment. This is the same technique I use to make sure employees internalize essential concepts. For example, in off-site planning meetings, I like to ask employees to think about how they will meet specific targets. As they think, plan, and discuss, they internalize the goal. They begin to visualize their individual actions to meet the goal. It becomes personal. And goals that become personal get done.

I also use this same technique around the organizational mission. I've learned that if I keep the mission statement short, I can use it better for internalization. A brief mission statement can be repeated daily in meetings and discussions so that employees hear it and know it's important. I also use it to reinforce and reward actions that support the company mission. As employees repeatedly hear the same consistent message, they know it's important, and they internalize it. This is a powerful tool to create organizational alignment in a mission-focused company.

Wrong Turn

It was a near-perfect May morning in Kings Bay, Georgia. The cool start to the day was replaced with warm, salty breezes coming off the marshes that surrounded the channel. We had left the tugboats behind, and all that remained was the familiar hint of their diesel exhausts. We were heading back to where the *Tennessee* was most comfortable, the Atlantic Ocean. Most of the problematic turns had been made. We were getting close to the point in the channel where it became wider, and the risk of hitting a buoy or running aground was lower.

I was in a good mood because I knew this deployment would be different. Despite the sadness of leaving my family for another three months, I was now an experienced member of the wardroom. I would be training and teaching the younger officers. I was also in a position that I had aspired to ever since I first dreamed of entering the submarine Navy: I was on the regular rotation to stand the officer of the deck watch. Every day on this patrol, I would spend six hours standing watch leading a nuclear submarine warship at sea. It was a young boy's dream come true.

Even more than that, I had been named the officer of the deck for the maneuvering watch, which meant that every time we took the *Tennessee* to sea or returned to port, I had the watch. Not only was I qualified, but I had become a capable watchstander as well. The captain and navigator put their trust in me for the most technically challenging role for an officer of the deck. The honor was not lost on me because they were literally putting their careers in my hands.

Most people don't know that the Navy has a zero-tolerance policy for hitting things. For good reason, the Navy believes that their ships should be operated in liquids, not solids. Running aground, hitting another ship, ramming a pier, or even hitting a buoy was grounds for dismissal. In most cases, the captain, navigator, and officer of the deck of any ship involved in one of these collision incidents are relieved of command. And the closer we operated to land, the more likely an incident like this could occur. Therefore, my performance as officer of the deck for the maneuvering watch had to be perfect. There was no room for error, especially when operating a 42-foot-wide warship in a 200-foot-wide channel with winds, shifting tides, and currents.

If you've ever operated a small boat, you know how tricky it is to maneuver in tight spaces. With one propeller, one rudder, and no brakes, you have to watch the currents and plan your moves in advance. Reversing the engine is your only means of slowing down, and if you slow down too much, you completely lose the ability to steer. Larger ships have two propellers to make it easier to make tight turns. Running one propeller forward and one in reverse can turn a ship quickly if needed. Many large cruise ships even have bow thrusters and rotatable propulsion pods, which give them the ultimate maneuverability to dock anywhere without using tugs.

The *Tennessee* didn't have any of these advancements and operated more like a small boat. We had one propeller, one rudder, and a rounded hull, making it extremely difficult to turn and maintain course at slow speeds. An Ohio-class submarine was at home under the ocean but a lumbering giant on the surface. Making it even more complicated was the fact that the officer of the deck didn't actually steer the boat from the bridge. The helmsman did that, and he was down in control with no view of the channel.

The only way the helmsman knew what to do was to listen to and follow the commands given by the officer of the deck. The helmsman was like a blindfolded driver on a narrow and dangerous mountain road, accelerating, braking, and steering based only on the commands given over the radio by someone sitting on a chair strapped to the roof. It was a delicate operation. One false move could run the boat aground or collide with a buoy or channel marker. This is why verbatim repeat-back was so critical. Operating in a narrow channel with little room for error meant the commands needed to be precise and carried out perfectly. This morning, they were not.

I watched as we passed a buoy on the starboard side, and I gave the command to take a right turn toward the South. The command was simple: "Right full rudder. Steady course 170." I expected to hear the repeat-back, see the rudder turn fully to the right, and the stern to swing away from the buoy on the starboard side. But the repeat-back was not verbatim. I heard the helmsman say, "Left full rudder. Steady course 170. Aye, sir." I turned and saw the rudder move to the left, and the stern start to swing towards the buoy. I reacted quickly and gave the command, "Wrong! Reverse your rudder! Right full rudder. Steady course 170." The reply came back, "Reverse my rudder. Right full rudder. Steady course 170. Aye, sir." The rudder quickly changed sides, kicking the stern safely away from the buoy. The *Tennessee* continued turning to the right as we came to the center of the channel on our journey's next leg. A collision with the buoy was narrowly avoided.

As we made our way to sea without any further incidents, I began to develop a deeper appreciation of the importance of verbatim repeat-back. When I first experienced it as a junior officer, I thought verbatim repeat-back was overkill. The risk that a watchstander would make a mistake or hear a command wrong seemed to be very low until it happened to me. Hearing the helmsman say the incorrect command gave me just enough time to realize something was wrong. Looking back at the rudder and seeing the boat moving toward the buoy confirmed the command was not being carried out correctly. I was able to correct the situation quickly to get back on course. Thankfully, the use of precise communication and verbatim repeat-back saved the day and proved its worth that morning.

Pump No Oil

It's always interesting to see the reaction when people find out I'm a submarine veteran. Most people say the same thing: "I could never do that." Some dig a little deeper. They want to know what it was like living on a submarine. They are curious. They want to know how we made oxygen and fresh water. They ask about the food and the beds. Eventually they get to the tricky questions, like what do we do with the trash and sewage? The answer always surprises them. It almost all goes overboard.

The U.S. Navy follows all maritime laws and has strict controls on what leaves the ship, but most waste does go overboard with two main exceptions: Plastic and oil never leave the ship. All plastic waste is stored for disposal when the boat returns to port. The crew even freezes all plastic waste exposed to food for the duration of the patrol. The main reason we kept plastics on board was because of the detrimental environmental effects. Oil was similar, but there was a military reason as well. Oil can give away a submarine's position.

Oil floats, and a sheen of oil can be seen by ships and aircraft for miles. Our primary mission was to remain undetected and be ready to deploy our weapons on command. Giving away our location because of an oil sheen would jeopardize that objective. It was mission-critical that the oil stayed in the boat, and everybody knew it. But in case there was any doubt, the Navy used verbatim repeat-back and repetition to ensure every watch officer and watchstander internalized this directive.

The officer of the deck was ultimately in charge of the ship while on watch, but it was the chief of the watch's job to control all the ship's systems. The chief of the watch maintained the trim of the boat by moving water throughout the boat and by pumping tanks overboard when needed. It required the officer of the deck's permission to pump any tank overboard, and the officer of the deck always provided one specific warning: "Pump no oil."

The interaction went something like this. The chief of the watch would ask, "Officer of the deck, request permission to pump #1 non-oily tank overboard." The officer of the deck would respond, "Pump #1 non-oily tank overboard; pump no oil." The chief of the watch would acknowledge the command, "Pump #1 non-oily tank overboard; pump no oil. Aye, sir." This exchange happened multiple times over a watch. As an officer, I probably gave the command "pump no oil" at least 1,000 times in my career. The Navy burned those three words into my core. I fully internalized that message.

The Navy knew how important it was to prevent an oil discharge. Not only was it bad for the environment and in violation of maritime rules, but it also went against our primary mission to remain undetected.

Using the command "pump no oil" as part of the verbatim repeat-back process ensured every watchstander and watch officer internalized this critical rule. Three words, repeated over and over, safeguarded our understanding and compliance. Verbatim repeat-back and repetition are powerful tools to internalize essential directives.

The Business World: Repetition and Mission

When I was stationed in Kings Bay and making patrols on the *Tennessee*, my wife was teaching at a small public elementary school in town. She had an amazing principal who understood the value of repetition. The school had a mission to maximize teaching time for each student. They wanted teachers to teach and not conduct other school business when the children were present. The principal used a simple way to communicate this mission; he used just four words over and over. In every meeting and interaction with his teachers, he would remind them to "get up and teach."

If teachers found themselves grading homework or working on lesson plans when the students were in the classroom, he wanted his words to remind them of what to do. He wanted them to put down their pens, get up out of their chairs, and teach students. He used four simple words, "get up and teach," to ensure each teacher understood and internalized the school's primary mission.

Like "pump no oil" for me, "get up and teach" was burned into my wife's core and was fully internalized. She understood how important it was to the organization's mission. All these years later, my wife still has those words echoing in her ears. Anytime she sits down in the classroom and is doing something other than teaching, her former boss's words come to her. If she's grading a paper or doing some administrative work, she hears his words, "get up and teach." So she does. She puts down her pen, gets up, and she teaches because she knows that's really what she's there to do. These four simple words have stood the test of time. A mission statement she will never forget.

Using repetition to internalize the mission statement is something I adopted in my role as CEO of a startup manufacturing business. I co-founded this business because, like my partners, I believed that customers were tired of the industry's existing suppliers. Lead times were long, prices were high, customer support was poor, and the buying process was complex. We wanted to change that, and that was our mission. We chose four simple words to communicate that mission. We reminded employees daily that we were a "different kind of supplier." Our objective was to provide something to the market that they couldn't get from the other guys.

For example, other suppliers took four to six weeks to ship their product; we did it in 24 hours. Other suppliers had complex buying processes, but you could order our products online and pay with a credit card if needed. If anything went wrong in the field, the other guys made it hard to get it resolved. We had people on the phone 24 hours a day to fix the problem as quickly as possible.

Our mission was to be different from the other vendors in our industry. Our simple mission statement was summed up in four words, to be a "different kind of supplier." We repeated this daily with every interaction with employees, so they understood and internalized the message. When an issue came up with a customer, I wanted my words echoing in the ears of every employee. If they ever started thinking like a big company, I wanted my words to remind them. I wanted them to choose a solution that would be different from the rest of the industry. I wanted them to understand, internalize, and live out what it meant to be a different kind of supplier. Like "pump no oil" and "get up and teach," being a "different kind of supplier" became engrained in my employees' core. Repetition is a powerful tool for creating a mission-minded organization.

When Close Enough Isn't Good Enough

Lying on my back and looking up at how the small work light made spaghetti-like shadows on the curved walls, a powerful emotion hit me. It wasn't fear. Given my current location and what I was working on, fear would have been a natural and acceptable reaction. Instead, what I felt was awe. In that tiny dark space with only the sounds of my breathing and an occasional muted echo from the outside world, I was suddenly mindful of the brilliance of submarine processes and procedures. Just the fact that I was in this place at this time spoke volumes.

There were hundreds of multicolored wires snaked through this cramped space and barely enough room to fit my 200-pound frame. I imagine this situation would create nightmares for the claustrophobic, but the confined space didn't bother me. The only thing concerning me was just above my head. Inches away from me was more explosive power than the atomic bombs dropped on the Japanese cities of Hiroshima and Nagasaki combined. I was profoundly aware I was working inside one of the deadliest weapons in the world. Yet, despite being a 26-year-old officer with only four years of experience, the Navy was confident I would perform this work flawlessly.

Today my job was to make sure all the wires in this part of the weapon were intact and each of the connections was solid. As the boat's missile officer, I inspected each of the 24 missiles before every patrol. The inspection wasn't just external either. Part of the assessment required me to open missile tube doors, remove access panels, and climb inside each missile just below the warheads to examine the wiring and connections.

When I signed up to be a submariner, I never expected to be doing anything like this. I kept thinking how surreal it was that the Navy would allow me to climb around the inside of a missile and trust that

I would execute my work flawlessly and consistently. It made me fully appreciate the Navy way of doing things.

I was following a carefully controlled procedure that demanded precision. A young sailor, a missile technician, worked directly with me to conduct this delicate operation. We followed a precise checklist, which he read aloud and I repeated. We completed every step with exactness. For example, before I entered each missile, I had to follow an exact procedure. I removed all metal from my body, took off my shoes, and applied tape along the zipper on my poopy suit. There could be no risk of damaging the missile or shorting out any circuit. After each step in the procedure, my assistant would inspect my actions to ensure I completed them correctly. It was a slow, methodical process designed to ensure perfect compliance to a precise procedure.

Just 50 years earlier, Manhattan Project scientists struggled to understand and harness this destructive power. They probably never imagined these weapons would one day become an essential deterrent to war in a protracted standoff between two superpowers. I'm sure they never thought that a relatively inexperienced guy like me would one day be crawling inside one of these devices. I know I never expected to be here, but this was just a typical day in the life of a submariner. Doing difficult and often dangerous work was commonplace. We were kept safe through rigorous training, precise communications, and detailed work procedures.

The Navy understood two things about dangerous work like we were doing that day. First, work procedures should be so clear and precise that a young officer and sailor could complete them correctly every time without incident. Second, the process needs to be painstakingly slow and meticulous such that it never became too familiar or routine. When it comes to actions that have deadly consequences, ones that put the crew's lives and the mission in jeopardy, close enough isn't good enough. Precision is mandatory.

THE BUSINESS WORLD: THE INSPECTOR

We were all nervous. This was a significant visit for our manufacturing operation. We'd worked hard to land this customer. The inspector who was about to arrive was the last person we needed to approve us as their primary vendor. We had prepared the factory for the visit, and the product was ready to go. Everything was perfect but we were all still feeling unsettled. Anything could happen today, and that would affect the future of our organization.

The production manager and I met the inspector upon his arrival in the plant's lobby. He was an older man with short gray hair and a stoic personality. We welcomed him with smiles but he remained sober. I realized this could be a long day for us.

We led him into our conference room, where I had assembled the management team. The managers introduced themselves, explained what they did, and talked about how long they'd been with the company. After that, I asked the inspector if he'd like to share a little bit about himself. The only thing he said was, "I'm just here to inspect the circuit breakers." That's it, nothing else. You could feel the tension in the room after his response. I figured the only thing I could do now was to get him out on the factory floor to see the product we had built for him. Maybe that would please him.

As we walked along, I tried without much success to engage in small talk with our visitor. I was hoping he would open up to me, but that didn't happen. One of the things I like to do when I'm meeting new people is to observe them. I try to find something about them I can use to break the ice. Are they wearing a school ring? Did it appear they were in the military? Do they have an accent? I always look for something I can use to find common ground and have a discussion on their terms. I especially needed it today with this inspector.

I kept glancing over at him, looking for a clue, anything I could find to break the ice. One thing I noticed was that he was wearing an identification badge from his company. More significantly, there were pins applied around the edges of the badge. When I looked closely, I saw the pins were from all of the various manufacturers he had visited. I instantly knew this was something I could use to connect with him. He was a pin collector, and he particularly liked pins from manufacturers in this industry. *That's perfect*, I thought. *I'll give him a pin from our company as a way to welcome him to our location and add to his collection.* While the inspector reviewed the circuit breaker with the production team, I went to see our marketing manager.

Before I tell you what happened next, I should tell you a little bit about this manufacturing plant. The factory was located in eastern South Carolina, in the heart of the deep South. As a New Englander, it was evident to me from day one that there was a different language being spoken at this plant. I could communicate with employees, but in most cases they had to talk slowly to me because I often struggled to understand their accents. I noticed they struggled at times to understand my accent as well.

The marketing manager was a delightful man, very outgoing, friendly, and always greeted me with a smile. If you're old enough to remember *The Andy Griffith Show*, he was a lot like Andy. He was a kind Southern gentleman who spoke with a rich, deep accent. I was able to track him down in his office, and he could see I was excited. I told him I had found a way to break the ice with the inspector. I explained that the inspector collected pins from companies he had visited, and I wanted to give him one from our company. The problem was I didn't think we had any pins in our marketing supply closet.

I was surprised when the marketing manager told me he had a box of pins with our logo on it and he would bring them to the conference room for the closeout meeting. I was excited to think we finally had something that could warm this icy inspector. I would present him with a pin as a memento of his visit to our plant. That would win him over.

At the closeout meeting, I learned the inspection on the circuit breaker went very well. The inspector didn't have any findings but he remained unemotional and kept his professional distance. Despite his demeanor, I took it as a good sign the visit was going well. We reviewed the full status of the inspection and discussed next steps.

During the discussion, my marketing manager walked in with the box. I smiled, thinking this was going to be the icing on the cake. The inspector would walk away knowing we made a high-quality product, *and* we cared about our customers. There was no way we could lose this business now. My marketing manager handed me the box, smiled, and said, "Here you go." I opened it up, and to my surprise, it wasn't a box of pins. It was a box of pens with our company logo on them.

I looked into the box and then back at him with a perplexed glance, but my marketing manager just smiled, thinking he had given me exactly what I wanted. I was confused. I wanted a pin but instead received a box of pens. I realized right away that my message was lost in translation. I learned the hard way that the Southern word for *pen* sounds a lot like *pin*. As it turned out, we didn't have any pins. All we had were pens. Unfortunately, I wasn't able to present the inspector with a meaningful gift during his visit and I wasn't able to break the ice as I'd hoped.

The good news is we ended up winning all the business from this customer. We also built a long-term, positive relationship with the inspector, who eventually warmed up to us on his next visit. After missing the opportunity to do something special for him the first time, I went out and purchased company pins and was able to present him with one on his second trip. This story had a good ending, but it shows the real problem when two people fail to communicate. When both parties assume the other person understood their message and fail to confirm that understanding, problems can occur. In this case, the miscommunication had limited consequences; however, sometimes the results can be costly.

Communicating with precision means ensuring people hear and understand what you are asking them to do. You should always verify that the other person understands the message and knows your intentions, especially with more-critical activities. That's the purpose of verbatim repeat-back. It's a careful and deliberate process designed to prevent miscommunications and ensure things get done the right way every time.

The Bottom Line

Key Points

- Verbatim repeat-back is a practice used in the Navy to ensure people execute orders perfectly.
- The practice confirms perfect alignment before execution.
- Verbatim repeat-back ensures understanding and creates internalization.
- Double-check with employees to verify there is a clear understanding of every assignment.
- Follow up early in projects to ensure there is continued understanding.
- Allow time for employees to internalize goals.
- Keep mission statements short and memorable to be used daily to promote internalization.
- Use repetition to create internalization.
- Increase formality in more-critical activities.

Tweetable Quotes

Tweet the following quotes with these hashtags: #allinthesameboat #communicatewithprecision

"Most misunderstandings occur when the task is first assigned."

"Following up on an assignment prevents miscommunication and costly mistakes."

"There is nothing more frustrating for both parties than an employee completing an important project incorrectly because he or she misunderstood the boss."

"Allow employees the time to internalize goals."

"Goals that become personal get done."

"As employees repeatedly hear the same consistent message, they know it's important, and they internalize it."

"Repetition creates internalization."

"When it comes to actions which have significant consequences, close enough isn't good enough."

Questions to Ponder

1. Can you think of a time when an employee completed a project incorrectly because there was a misunderstanding when you first assigned the task? How can you prevent that from reoccurring?

2. What are you doing to allow employees to internalize goals and objectives?

3. How are you reinforcing your mission statement daily?

4. How can you apply the concepts of verbatim repeat-back to your organization?

Chapter 4. Eliminate Failure as an Option

Sliding silently through the dark ocean, sometimes you forget where you are,
Until you remember there's no moon, not even a glimmering star.
They all wait above you in silence, for the boat to once more breach the waves,
In a rush of wild water and motion, escaping a watery grave.

– Bob MacPherson, *The Old Submariner*

Test Depth

We had been at periscope depth for nearly 30 minutes. I was the officer of the deck on the scope enjoying a little "eyeball liberty." There wasn't much to see this morning, just a calm ocean and a clear blue sky. The captain wanted me to make sure there were no other ships in the area. The maneuver we were about to conduct was designed to test our ability to get to the surface quickly in an emergency. Our actions would send the *Tennessee* hurtling uncontrolled to the surface, so we needed the area to be fully clear before performing this critical drill. Satisfied we were alone in this part of the Atlantic, I commanded the diving officer to bring the boat down to test depth.

Test depth is the maximum depth at which a submarine can operate in normal peacetime circumstances. The Navy verifies this during sea trials after initial construction and every major overhaul. It is considered the deepest depth where a submarine can operate safely. For the U.S. Navy, this depth is considered classified, and no submariner worth their salt will tell you what it is. However, the Navy's Submarine Force Pacific website states that Ohio-class submarines like the *Tennessee* can attain depths in excess of 800 feet. That's where we were headed.

Making the trip to test depth is always a memorable experience. It's considered a rite of passage for new crew members and a bragging right for veterans. A sailor's cumulative time at test depth is the ultimate measure of submarine experience. Every young submariner has heard this colorful expression more than once from a salty old chief petty officer: "Son, I've spent more time on the shitter at test depth than you've been in the Navy." Yes, submariners have a strange sense of humor.

I still remember the first time I made the journey to test depth. I wasn't even a commissioned officer yet. I was a young midshipman on a summer training cruise. I was assigned to the *USS Guitarro*, a Sturgeon-class fast-attack submarine based in San Diego. The officers on board sent me to the torpedo room for my first trip to test depth. One of the experienced sailors tied a string tight across the compartment.

As we descended, I listened with shock as the hull creaked,

groaned, and strained under the Pacific Ocean's crushing pressure. I watched in horror as the string continued to become slack the deeper we went. Every 30 feet of depth added another 15 pounds per square inch of pressure on the hull, and I could see and hear the effects of that pressure. I remember thinking that test depth was a dangerous place, and being crushed in a submarine at sea would be a terrible way to die.

Years later, the creaking and groaning of the *Tennessee* as she descended was now a familiar sound. As an experienced submariner, I was used to it. The reverberations of unrelenting sea pressure having its way with the high-strength steel hull didn't bother me much. I had made this journey dozens of times. I respected the depths but didn't fear them. I knew what the boat could take, and I knew how to get it to the surface if necessary. Still, I kept a close eye on the depth gauge. Like me, everyone in control watched as the numbers on the indicator continued to increase. After several minutes, we reached test depth and leveled out.

The maneuver we were about to conduct was an emergency main ballast tank blow, also known as an emergency blow. This is a procedure where high-pressure air is forced into the main ballast tanks. The water in the tanks is rapidly replaced with air. The boat becomes instantly buoyant and shoots to the surface like a basketball from the bottom of a swimming pool… only the *Tennessee* was a 560-foot, 19,000-ton basketball. An emergency blow is a wild ride, better than anything at Disney World.

The emergency blow procedure was made famous in the 1990 submarine movie *Hunt for Red October*. In one scene, the fictional *USS Dallas* uses an emergency blow to escape a Russian torpedo. As the torpedo closes in on the *Dallas*, Lieutenant Commander Thompson directs the diving officer to "put us on the roof" and initiates an emergency blow. As the *Dallas* rapidly ascends to the surface, Thompson famously mutters, "Come on, Big D. Fly!" And fly she did.

In this iconic scene, the audience is treated to actual filmed footage of a nuclear submarine breaching the surface on the big screen. The raw, visceral power of an emergency blow is on full display as nearly a third of the submarine soars out of the water during the violent maneuver. If you haven't seen the movie in a while, you should go back and watch this part. The movie was filmed before the widespread use of computer-generated imagery (CGI), so you see actual footage of a real submarine during an emergency ascent. In fact, the fictional *USS Dallas* was played by the real-life Los Angeles-class attack submarine *USS Houston*, which made more than 40 emergency blows for the rehearsal and filming of the movie.

Once we were steady at test depth with no close contacts, I obtained permission from the captain to conduct an emergency blow. When we were ready to go, I gave the command "Dive, emergency surface!" which was responded to smartly by the diving officer with "Emergency surface, dive, aye!" The diving officer then carried out a perfect set of orders. The helmsman and planesman were directed to accelerate to flank speed and put a full rise on the planes to reach a 40 degree up bubble. The chief of the watch was ordered to sound the diving alarm and pass the word on the 1MC of "Emergency Surface!" Throughout the boat, I heard the announcement followed by three blasts of the dive alarm, "Ahh-OO-gah! Ahh-OO-gah! Ahh-OO-gah!"

The diving officer then gave the final command: "Chief of the watch, emergency blow!" After a verbatim repeat-back, the chief of the watch stood up and energetically threw open the two emergency blow activator handles. I should point out that submariners affectionately call these handles "chicken switches." I don't know the true origin story for this nickname, but I imagine a submarine sailor at some point probably said, "What? Are you chickening out?" And it stuck. As I mentioned, submariners have an interesting sense of humor.

The deafening roar of air rushing to main ballast tanks drowned out all noise in control as the *Tennessee* quickly reached a 40 degree rise. I could see everyone leaning forward and holding on to anything to steady themselves as we rocketed to the surface. The diving officer yelled out the ever-decreasing depth as we quickly passed through hundreds of feet of ocean. My job as officer of the deck was to hang on and enjoy the short ride to the surface.

When we broke the surface, the *Tennessee* flew out of the water, exposing her full bow, then crashed back down to the surface like a breaching humpback whale. Crew members in the bow of the boat had the best ride, feeling weightless as the boat dropped from 40 degree to level in a matter of seconds. The *Tennessee* shuddered and rocked, then settled. An eerie quiet replaced the loud noise of rushing air throughout the boat. We had safely reached the surface.

This was a maneuver we had practiced dozens of times. It was second nature to every experienced crew member, and for a good reason. If anything ever happened, we all knew the only way we would survive as a crew was to reach the surface.

There is a universal rule in submarining: Surfaces must always equal dives. While this might sound obvious, it is something every submariner takes very seriously. When it comes to getting to the surface, failure is not an option. You might be surprised to learn that there is no practical way to save a submarine crew if the boat goes down in the depths we usually operated. The ocean is a very deep and unforgiving place. If something goes wrong, in all likelihood the entire crew will be lost. Every sailor knows there is no other option; you must reach the surface.

The world was reminded of the dangers of submarine operations with the tragic loss of the Argentinian submarine *San Juan* and her crew of 44 sailors in November 2017. When she disappeared, a search and rescue operation that involved more than 4,000 personnel from 13 countries failed to find any sign of the missing submarine and her crew.

It took more than a year to locate the ill-fated sub. She was found resting on the ocean floor at a relatively shallow depth of just 3,000 feet. She had failed to reach the surface, which resulted in the tragic loss of all hands.

My experience in the Navy taught me that some goals are simply non-negotiable. There are objectives in every organization where the possibility of failure must be eliminated. The outcome must be achieved regardless of the circumstances. If you think about your business, you can probably name at least one goal that fits this description. As leaders, it's our job to make sure these objectives are always met.

To do this, we must start with the mindset that the goal is non-negotiable. We need to create a culture that attacks problems with the same attitude and tenacity as a submarine crew trying to reach the surface. And we need systems and processes to ensure flawless execution. Building a mindset, culture, and systems that can consistently achieve targets regardless of the challenges is powerful. It's also not easy to do. It takes a conscious, all-encompassing effort to create an organization like this. To understand how the Navy created this culture, we need to look back at the creation of the SUBSAFE program.

SUBSAFE LEGACY

It's hard to comprehend how deep the Atlantic Ocean is. Depths are around 500 feet close to shore, but past the continental shelf the ocean floor drops sharply beyond 12,000 feet. The deepest parts of the Atlantic are more than 27,000 feet deep… That's five miles, which makes the Atlantic as deep as Mount Everest is tall. And unlike the deep-diving research submarines, which are designed to reach depths of 15,000+ feet, military submarines operate closer to the surface in just 800 feet of water. There is no strategic advantage for operating much deeper. It would be cost-prohibitive to build a large submarine that could withstand those depths. The *Tennessee* and submarines like her cruised in the shallowest parts of the water column with the vast abyss of the Atlantic Ocean always looming deep beneath the hull.

Over the years the U.S. Navy has designed and deployed various systems and methods to rescue submariners if they are unable to reach the surface. And they needed to because underwater operations remained a dangerous business. From 1915 to 1963, sixteen American submarines were lost to non-combat-related causes. For years the Navy's primary focus was on developing better methods of rescue. All that changed when the lead boat of an advanced new class of nuclear-powered attack submarines was lost in 1963. On April 10, while diving to test depth just 200 miles off the New England coast, the *USS Thresher* had a casualty. They reported "minor difficulties" but had a "positive up-angle," and they were "attempting to blow." Sadly, that was the last thing that was ever heard from her. She failed to reach the surface, and America lost her first nuclear submarine. The *Thresher's* wreckage was later found on the ocean floor in 8,400 feet of water with a loss of all 129 submariners and shipyard personnel.

The tragic and shocking loss of America's most modern nuclear-powered submarine prompted a significant turning point in the mindset of how the Navy thought about submarine rescues. An in-depth study of the *Thresher* accident determined that, although the submarine's basic design was sound, changes were needed. Steps needed to be taken to improve hull integrity and the submarines' ability to recover from casualties and still reach the surface. This study concluded that the best way to save a submarine crew was to get the sub to the surface even after a significant casualty. This concept was a new mindset. Failure to reach the surface was no longer an option. That failure mode had to be systematically eliminated. It was the tragedy of the *Thresher* that led to the most successful safety program the Navy ever created, the SUBSAFE program.

The *Thresher* disaster was caused by a failure of silver-brazed joints on piping, which caused flooding in the engine room. The resulting saltwater spray damaged electrical equipment, which caused the reactor to shut down. Without propulsion, the only way to get to the surface was an emergency blow, but *Thresher*'s systems failed. Moisture in the emergency blow piping had frozen and blocked air from reaching the ballast tanks. The crew couldn't get *Thresher* to the surface. The submarine systems weren't good enough to save the crew during a flooding casualty at test

Eliminate Failure as an Option

depth. The Navy created SUBSAFE to fix this.

The SUBSAFE program addressed all areas of submarine design, materials, fabrication, and testing. This program raised the bar on how submarines were built, maintained, and operated. The Navy was determined to learn from *Thresher*. Eventually, only subs which reached and maintained their SUBSAFE certification would be allowed to conduct submerged operations. The Navy created a culture where every submariner and shipyard worker was trained in this comprehensive quality and safety program. SUBSAFE certification covered all the systems exposed to sea pressure and those needed for flooding recovery. The work done by shipyard workers and the materials used in these systems was tightly controlled to ensure nothing could fail. Perfection was now the expectation.

The program was enormously successful. Since SUBSAFE began in 1963, only one U.S. submarine has been lost, the *USS Scorpion*, which was not yet SUBSAFE certified. The nuclear-powered *Scorpion* disappeared under mysterious circumstances in 1968. While the exact cause of the *Scorpion* disaster is still unknown, it's clear the *Thresher* lessons have made U.S. submarine operations much safer. More than 200 nuclear-powered U.S. submarines since *Thresher* have safely steamed millions of hours under the surface for more than 50 years without the loss of a single submarine. On September 26, 2019, a memorial for the *USS Thresher* crew was dedicated at Arlington National

Cemetery. The words on the memorial state, "In honor of the 129 men lost aboard the *USS Thresher* (SSN-593) and their SUBSAFE legacy."

The lesson of the Navy's SUBSAFE program is that non-negotiable goals start with a mindset. It then takes a determined, all-hands effort to build a culture that eliminates failure. It also requires significant time and effort to develop systems and processes to ensure the outcome is achieved regardless of the circumstances. All this is needed if we expect perfection as the minimum standard.

While it took a tragedy for the Navy to build this mindset, culture, and system, leaders in any organization can achieve similar results. It takes a relentless, unwavering commitment to reinforce non-negotiable goals. For example, in one business I led, we had a non-negotiable commitment that all requests for quotes (RFQs) would be responded to on the same day. That meant that no matter how many RFQs were received in a given day, each one would get a response that same day without fail. That commitment meant that if we were swamped with requests, one or more employees would stay late to ensure we always maintained a perfect daily response. Just like reaching the surface, our goal was 100% performance every day. We eliminated failure as an option.

NUKE SCHOOL

Florida's heat and humidity in July are brutal, but it wasn't the weather that was bothering me. I was spending my days in a 70 degree air-conditioned classroom and my evenings in a 60 degree air-conditioned study room. I was in the fight of my life. The harsh reality of choosing a career as a nuclear submarine officer was hitting me like a Category 5 hurricane, and I struggled to hold on. My dreams were unraveling before my eyes.

After graduating from college and receiving my commission as a naval officer, I was assigned to my first duty station, the U.S. Naval Nuclear Power School in Orlando, also known as Nuke School. This school was the first step on the long journey to become a nuclear submarine officer. I had graduated earlier in the year with a degree in Mechanical Engineering from Worcester Polytechnic Institute (WPI) in Massachusetts. I graduated with distinction, but it wasn't due to my classroom grades. I had worked hard and received the highest marks on my undergraduate research projects, which counted for special honors at graduation. I was never the smartest guy in any of my classes, but I was always persistent and hard-working, which showed up in my project work. Fortunately for me, that mattered at WPI.

I was confident that I could make it to the submarine fleet if I could get through Nuke School. Nuclear Prototype Training and

Submarine School would follow Nuke School; both were more hands-on and more up my alley. Nuke School, however, was all classroom and pure academics. This was going to be a real challenge for me.

I knew there would be some intelligent guys at Nuke School, but I had no idea! My class was made up of the smartest guys from every top university across the country, including my roommate. He had achieved a perfect 4.0 GPA in college and graduated with a degree in nuclear engineering. He was sharp, experienced in nuclear power, and belonged here. I wasn't sure I did.

I had a classic case of imposter syndrome. People with imposter syndrome suffer from what *Harvard Business Review* defines as "chronic self-doubt and a sense of intellectual fraudulence." From my first day at Nuke School, I felt like a fraud, like someone had made a mistake and let me in. I never thought I belonged with people this smart. I remembered what I told my parents when they called to see how I was doing: "I'm surrounded by the best of the best, and I'm in way over my head. I've finally met my match."

The rules to make it to graduation at Nuke School were simple: Maintain a GPA greater than 2.5 and don't fail two of the major subject final exams. I quickly made this my Nuke School mantra: "2.5 and survive." I knew I wasn't going to be the honor graduate; I just needed to make it to graduation. I needed to get through this school. The truth of the matter was, I didn't have a Plan B.

Since my sophomore year in high school, I had dreamed of becoming a naval officer on a nuclear submarine. I had decent enough grades and managed to get a four-year ROTC scholarship to an excellent engineering school. My college performance was good enough for me to get accepted into the Navy's nuclear power program, but now I was facing my most significant test. I needed to survive Nuke School and graduate in order to continue pursuing my dream. Honestly, I had no idea what I would do if I failed out. The idea of being assigned to some old frigate out of Norfolk scared the hell out of me. (Apologies to all the old frigate sailors who are reading this.) That's not what I wanted to do with my life, so I decided early on that I would make it through Nuke School. It was a mindset. No matter what, I would graduate. It was a non-negotiable goal, and failure was not an option.

The first month of Nuke School was brutal. It was clear they were trying to weed people out of the program. There was a 40% attrition rate at the time, and I was determined not to be one of those left behind. I remember getting my first math assignment back. I made a minor calculation error on a paper with 30 problems on it. I had shown all my work, praying to the "god of partial credit" as I did for years as an undergraduate. The instructor marked that problem with a massive red *X* and put an *F* on the assignment. I was furious and stormed out of the classroom to meet with the instructor.

I showed her the assignment and asked why she failed me for a simple calculation error. She sternly looked at me and said, "One simple error, and now the reactor is shut down at sea. You have just put the entire crew at risk." I realized then that Nuke School wasn't anything like college. The god of partial credit wasn't allowed on this base. Mistakes weren't tolerated. They had a mission to train officers who would not make simple errors. I had a lot to learn.

The instructors were also fond of marking assignments and tests with acronyms like **GCE**, which we learned stood for "gross conceptual error," or **BOB** for "better off blank." It felt like they were saying, "You're an idiot and don't belong here." If a student made even the smallest mistake, it was treated severely. They were trying to send a message that mistakes were not tolerated. I remember my roommate received an assignment back that was marked **GCE to the GCE power (GCE^{GCE})**, which was meant as a complete insult.

I started with a decent GPA and I was beginning to think I had a shot, but Nuke School hadn't even warmed up yet. As I soon learned, the topics just kept getting more complicated, and the pace and volume of information kept increasing. I soon found I was drinking from a fire hose and trying to retain as much as I could. As the weeks and months continued, my GPA declined.

I continued to remind myself of my mantra, "2.5 and survive." At some point, I taped a small chart to the corner of my desk to track my

GPA per week. The vertical axis of the graph went from 4.0 to 2.5. As Nuke School continued, the slope of my GPA graph continued to trend down. During a long lecture one day, I drew a crude aircraft carrier at the end of the chart at the 2.5 line. I told myself that my goal was to land on that carrier after six months. I knew if I dropped below 2.5, I would crash and burn into the ocean. It was a daily reminder of my mission.

Like most students at Nuke School, my GPA fell to the point I was placed on mandatory study hours. This wasn't like college; we couldn't take anything home to study. When you were on compulsory study hours, you had to physically log your hours in at the Nuke School study room, or what we used to call "the cooler." The study room was kept at a perpetual 60 degrees – it was freezing in there. The rumor was they kept it cold to keep students from falling asleep. I assumed they did it to torture us. It didn't matter to me. They could turn it down to 32 degrees – I was going to do whatever it took to graduate.

After about four months of Nuke School, I finally figured out a method to succeed. There was far too much information for me to try to learn and fully understand. It was impossible (for me) to digest that much information. However, I began seeing that each instructor would stress certain aspects of each subject they deemed critical or essential. I zeroed in on those crucial pieces of information. Instead of trying to understand them fully, I would commit them to my short-term memory, calling it my "I believe" process. I had a drawing of a little button taped to my desk that said, "I believe." Whenever a new concept was introduced and I didn't have the time to understand it fully, I would push the button and say, "Okay, I believe it," and I would commit it to my short-term memory.

It might sound like the absolute worst way to learn any subject, but this method worked perfectly for me. Remember, I was in the "2.5 and survive" club. Eventually this system got my grades up enough to make it to the final exam. During that test I spit out everything I knew and by some miracle I passed. I landed that plane right on the carrier deck. I don't remember my final GPA at Nuke Power School, but it couldn't have been much higher than 2.55. It didn't matter because I graduated. Getting through Nuke School was a non-negotiable goal. Failure was not an option, and I found a way to graduate. Even to this day, it's one of my proudest accomplishments.

When you choose a goal that's non-negotiable, when you eliminate failure as an option, you find a way to meet that goal every time. Whether it's reaching the surface in a submarine, responding to daily RFQs, or getting through Nuke School, deciding not to fail is a choice. It's a mindset that is powerful for consistent performance.

THE BUSINESS WORLD: LOST IN TRANSLATION

The Korean Air Boeing 747 jumbo jet touched down at the Gimhae International Airport on Busan's western end. After the long flight, I was ready to get out and stretch my legs. While I had traveled extensively, I had never been to South Korea. I was excited to be here and eager to get on with the mission at hand.

We had come here for one purpose. We were visiting a legendary manufacturing plant. The operation wasn't famous outside our company, but it certainly was within. It was considered the best of the best. I was working for a global welding equipment manufacturing company. At the time, I was responsible for two manufacturing plants in the United States. We were in the process of implementing lean manufacturing, and we had come to the far side of the world to benchmark the preeminent performing plant in the company. What we learned here would be used to improve our factories in the U.S.

I was traveling with two VIPs. They weren't vice presidents or board members; they were two workers from our Pennsylvania manufacturing plant. Both were longtime employees and members of the union at that facility. For years upper management had told the union how good the South Korean operation was and how the American plants needed to improve their performance. I invited them to come on this trip with me so we could learn together. I wanted all of us to see what was so good about this business and wanted them to come back with a message of what was possible. We were all going to learn something important from this trip.

When we arrived at the plant, we were given a translator to communicate with management and the facility's workers. On our initial tour, we were all impressed. The employees were proficient and hard-working. The plant was clean and well organized. It was evident they had implemented many of the lean manufacturing concepts. The plant was well lit, orderly, and they seemed to be very efficient. It was apparent why they had the best performance in the company.

We began to study their metrics. We met with various managers around the plant to review their performance numbers in quality, scrap, safety, productivity, and production. We wanted to learn as much as we could to compare their performance to ours. I had a long list of KPIs I was looking to benchmark and, in every category, we found that the South Korean operation was better than ours. This was shaping up to be a valuable trip.

Then came a surprise I hadn't expected when I tried to study their delivery performance. Most manufacturing plants measure delivery performance with an on-time delivery metric. It's usually calculated as the number of products shipped on time by the "promise date" divided by the number of units shipped. Our goal was to ship more than 90% of our products on time, and we were running in the high 80s. When

I asked one of the South Korean managers what his on-time delivery performance was, I could see he didn't understand the question. I repeated the question several times to my translator, who relayed the question again to the manager.

It was clear I was not getting through. I explained how we measured on-time delivery and asked for their information. I was looking for their number. Were they at 80%, 85%, 90% or higher? I was curious. I asked again, and the translator translated. My South Korean counterpart continued to look puzzled. I finally asked, "How do you measure your delivery performance? What is your goal for on-time delivery?" It was at that point he finally understood the question and had an answer. He spoke very clearly to my translator, who then translated the message to me: "Why would you ever ship late to a customer? Why would you not fulfill your promise?"

His words hit me square in the chest. They didn't measure delivery performance because they always delivered on time. Delivering products to customers as promised was a non-negotiable goal. It was a mindset. Failure was not an option when it came to deliveries. When this plant pledged to ship a product to a customer on a specific date, they sent it on time, every time. I immediately thought back to my days on the boat and our non-negotiable goal. We reached the surface every time. And come to think of it, we didn't measure it either; we just did it.

In this world-class manufacturing plant on the other side of the world, I saw a non-negotiable goal in action. They deliver on time, 100% of the time, without fail. They had built a culture and a system that was designed not to fail. They didn't make a shipping promise they couldn't deliver on, and their employees knew this goal was non-negotiable. It was a mindset with a culture and system to back it up. What struck me is they couldn't even understand the concept of measuring on-time delivery performance. It was eye-opening for both the team I was traveling with and me.

We understood why this plant was so good. They had the right mindset, culture, and systems, which was an impactful lesson. Like my Nuclear Power School experience, committing to a non-negotiable goal is a mindset, and they were truly committed. But they also built the team, culture, and systems to deliver consistent performance. They didn't promise anything they couldn't deliver. They valued performance over excuses and were committed to keeping promises. Unlike our plants, they didn't have to analyze every month to determine why they were late – they were never late. Non-negotiable goals are powerful, and any business can implement them. Probably the most common one I see in manufacturing plants is safety.

Safety, like any other non-negotiable goal, begins with a mindset. Leaders first commit to worker safety. In most cases, leaders quickly embrace the goal of preventing serious injuries and deaths at their workplace. As a safety culture begins to grow and thrive in a company, the goal shifts. As more employees focus on safety, it soon becomes the goal that even minor injuries in the workplace must be avoided. A zero-tolerance mindset for unsafe acts is created, and safety becomes a non-negotiable goal. It doesn't take long for everyone to realize safety is not just good for people; it's also good for business.

This was precisely the mindset that Paul O'Neill put in place at Alcoa, the world's eighth-largest producer of aluminum. When he took over as CEO in 1987, he announced, "I intend to make Alcoa the safest company in America. I intend to go for zero injuries." And that's what he did. O'Neill put in place the mindset, culture, and systems to make this happen. After the safety plan was fully rolled out and internalized by employees, its worker injury rate fell to 1/20 of the U.S. average. Many facilities went years without a work injury. By the time he retired in 2000, Alcoa had become one of the world's safest companies. O'Neill decided that it was no longer an option that employees were hurt on the job. Safety became a non-negotiable goal, and failure wasn't an option.

NOT ON MY WATCH

It was a typical Saturday morning filled with maintenance and a few casualty drills. As one of the more experienced junior officers, I was part of the drill team responsible for running and evaluating the crew's performance during these simulated casualties. Today we were running

Eliminate Failure as an Option

one of my favorite drills, which assessed how the crew responded to a disaffected crewman. The plan was to evaluate the response to a crew member trying to tamper with equipment in the missile compartment.

As the team prepared to initiate the drill, I stationed myself by the hatch outside of the crew's mess. I wanted to see how the sailors on this deck would perform during this scenario. I was there for just five minutes when the announcement came over the 1MC. The drill had begun. The voice on the 1MC stated there was a disaffected crewman in the missile compartment. The crew sprang to life and went to their assigned duty stations. Many sailors sprinted to the small-arms locker, where they were issued 45-caliber handguns and 12-gauge shotguns. The hatches to the missile compartment were shut and "dogged," and guards were placed at each hatch.

There was a young seaman assigned to the hatch outside of the crew's mess where I was stationed. He was new to the boat, so it was an excellent chance to evaluate his training. He seemed to understand his assignment. I watched him carefully as he secured the hatch and stood guard with the 12-gauge shotgun he was issued. The crew was trained not to let anyone pass through any hatches until the disaffected crewman was found and apprehended. This young sailor was about to get the ultimate test.

Most days, when we ran drills, the captain monitored the response from the control room. He relied on the boat's drill team to tell him how the crew performed during the event. Occasionally, he would wander out to where the casualty was taking place to monitor the crew's performance himself. That was the case today. The captain was in the missile compartment for the start of this drill and was watching the crew's response first-hand.

The hatches to the missile compartment, like the one I was observing, were solid steel except for a small six-inch viewing window. Once they were shut and "dogged," there was no way to get through unless someone on the other side opened it for you. As I watched the young sailor outside the crew's mess, there was a sudden pounding on the hatch. Someone was trying to get through. I looked at the small window and noticed it was the captain. I guess he was trying to come into the forward compartment to observe the response from another vantage point. The seaman guarding the door didn't even look to see who it was. He stood his ground and yelled, "Go around! This hatch is secured!" Well done, I thought. His training was good.

I could see the captain wasn't playing, though. He wasn't just testing the sailor. He genuinely wanted to move into the forward compartment to observe the drill. When the sailor didn't open the hatch, the captain got angry and pounded even harder on the hatch. The seaman remained unfazed. He stood his ground and just yelled louder, "Go around! This hatch is secured!" *Very interesting*, I thought. *This sailor is not backing down.*

Through the small viewing window, I could tell the captain was getting agitated. He wanted to pass through this hatch but the young sailor would not let that happen on his watch. I started to smile, thinking about what I was observing. Here was the most junior sailor on the boat telling the most senior officer what to do. And the junior sailor was correct. He was following his training correctly.

As I continued to watch the window, I saw the captain bend down to try to see who was responsible for blocking his passage. He was looking for someone to blame for his frustration. I watched as the captain's angry eye and bushy eyebrow filled the entire viewing window. His eyeball darted back and forth, looking for the source of his annoyance. It looked like something from a cartoon, and I couldn't help but laugh at what I saw play out.

The enraged captain pounded even louder on the hatch to try getting the sailor's attention. But the young sailor stood his ground and refused to yield, exactly how he'd been trained. The seaman ignored the angry eyeball and the constant pounding then yelled at the top of his voice, "Go around, motherf***er!!" As his blunt words echoed down the passageway outside of the crew's mess, I started to laugh out loud. I couldn't believe what just happened. This kid just chewed out our commanding officer.

The young sailor looked at me with a confused look. He had no idea why I was laughing, and he had no idea who was on the other side of that hatch. I saw the captain shake his head in disbelief and walk off. He knew he was defeated. He wasn't getting through this hatch until after the drill was over. In my observation notebook, I gave the young sailor credit for standing his ground and executing his duties flawlessly during this drill. I just wondered what the captain would say when it was all over.

I learned later that day that the captain sought out the seaman. Instead of reprimanding the young man, however, he praised him for doing the right thing by not letting him or anyone else pass. The captain recognized the young sailor's actions because he refused to compromise his duty to defend that hatch. The captain understood that the rules for handling this situation applied to him as well.

That day I witnessed what it looks like to have non-negotiable goals. There was no way that sailor would let anyone through that door, not even the captain. He was trained to lock down that door and not let anyone through. Failure was not an option. When you have a mindset, a system, and the training to back up non-negotiable goals, your team will execute them with precision every time.

THE BUSINESS WORLD: PROJECT BEARS

"Why are we even in this business?" That was the question I was just asked by the global president of our division. It came in the middle of a business review. I had just finished presenting the financial numbers of the business I had recently been assigned to. The numbers weren't good, and everyone knew it. When I corrected the profits to take out the effect of raw material hedging, it showed the business hadn't made money in four years. Something needed to change. As the new general manager, the pressure was on me.

The president liked to show he was a decisive leader. He was German and had spent most of his career in engineering. As a natural problem solver, he launched right into a solution. "There is too much high-cost American labor in your production costs. You need to move production to China." I was worried about this type of knee-jerk response and was prepared with an answer.

I reminded the president that several other competitors had moved their production to China only to see their market share rapidly erode. I felt there was still value in having the product built in the States. I asked for the opportunity to put together a plan to turn this business around without outsourcing production to China. He reluctantly agreed under one condition: that I radically reduce the amount of high-cost labor in our production costs. Even though I wasn't exactly sure how I would do that, I agreed to his terms.

I was given three months to work with the management team to create a plan to turn this business around. The plan had to reduce the high-cost labor content and improve profits. If we couldn't figure it out, the division was fully prepared to move the entire production line to

China. I knew that would be a disaster for our employees and our sales. The future of the business depended on our ability to create and execute a plan. On the trip back from the business review, I made a decision that I would not fail in this mission. I refused to see this business become another statistic. We had to figure out a way to save it. Failure was not an option.

I began by presenting the challenge to the management team, and the reaction was about what I expected. They had already worked hard to reduce the product's local labor content to only about 20 minutes. Any further reduction was, in their minds, virtually impossible. That first meeting ended without any real plan to move forward. I was beginning to think it was a lost cause. My desire to keep production in the United States was looking like an impossible pipe dream. What I didn't realize at the time was that I had planted a seed with the management team, which took just a few days to grow.

"Panama!" the supply chain manager exclaimed. "That's the answer." I was confused. In our second meeting to discuss the business turnaround plan, he had just thrown me a curveball. The answer was simple, the supply chain manager explained. He was already purchasing many of the individual components from China and India. He could bring them all into the west coast of Panama, build them into subassemblies in a free-trade zone in Panama City, then ship them out to the east coast to our factory in North Carolina. This solution would shift much of the labor cost to Panama but still allow final assembly in the United States.

It was an interesting idea but I had my doubts. What did we know about doing business in Panama? How could we set up a subassembly operation in a country I had never even been to? How could we manage the logistics?

Even though I thought the idea was crazy, I decided the only way to prove or disprove it was to send a team to Panama to investigate the concept further. So I sent the supply manager and manufacturing engineering manager to Panama on a fact-finding mission. Whatever they uncovered would either support this idea or debunk it right away. It seemed like a long shot, but it was the only solution that we hadn't yet tried. The trip would determine the future of this business.

Upon their return, I was pleasantly surprised by what they had discovered. There were many outfits in Panama doing this type of work for American companies. They had the logistics and processes already figured out. Our team had narrowed it down to two Panamanian operations with the experience and capacity to handle our businesses. The more I reviewed the numbers, looked at photos of their operations, and considered the timing, the more I was convinced this could work. All I needed to do now was persuade the division president.

I spent the next two months working with the local management team refining the plan to shift all of the subassembly production to

Panama. I tried to anticipate the concerns of the division president. We knew he preferred to move the entire operation to China. We weren't sure how he would react to our out-of-the-box proposal. To our surprise, however, he liked the concept and quickly approved our Panama plan. He saw the value in what we were trying to do, and he gave us his full support. We now had the green light to move forward.

We called the plan Project Bears. The company had a tradition of giving nicknames to confidential projects. The first letter of the project name usually had significance. In our case, the "B" in Bears just stood for Plan B. This was our plan to save the business. We knew if we failed, the president would probably enact Plan C and move the business to China. We all understood that Project Bears had to succeed.

It took an entire year to complete all of the activities of Project Bears. Equipment had to be moved and set up in Panama; suppliers needed to be trained and qualified; logistics had to be set up and coordinated; and inventory had to be put in place. It was hard work, but we each knew the consequences of failure. We completed the project on time, and by the end of the first year we began operating the new Project Bears supply chain. In a few short months we saw a drastic reduction in the high-cost labor. Final production time was reduced to just 90 seconds and profits improved to single digits.

The other thing that happened during this time is that customers recognized that we were one of only two manufacturers still doing final assembly in the United States. This gave us flexibility and shorter lead times compared to the competition. As a result, customers rewarded us with even more business. Both our top and bottom lines improved in the first six months after completing Project Bears. In the next six months the situation got even better.

Sales and profits continued to grow at a record pace. A year after completing Project Bears, our company was both the market share leader and was producing a double-digit profit margin. We had not only saved the business, but our efforts were also considered a massive success inside the division. We had accomplished something that was genuinely out-of-the-box and colossally successful. We ignored the calls to move production to China and, instead, developed a new way of operating a factory in a high-labor-cost market. Eventually other businesses in our division benchmarked our efforts to learn from our success.

I attribute the success of Project Bears to the local management team's creative thinking, fueled by the fact that we all had our backs against the wall. Failure to deliver a plan to improve the business would have been a disaster. Outsourcing production to China would have meant the end of this business as we knew it. Instead, we chose to eliminate failure as an option. We chose a creative solution to improve the business drastically, and we were rewarded with extraordinary success. Often the fear of failure can motivate you to your absolute best performance.

THE BOTTOM LINE

Key Points

- Some goals are simply non-negotiable.
- Any organization can implement non-negotiable goals.
- Non-negotiable goals are objectives that must be achieved regardless of the circumstances.
- Establishing a non-negotiable goal starts with a mindset.
- It takes a determined, all-hands effort to build a culture that is not willing to allow failure.
- Systems, processes, and training are required to ensure flawless execution.

Tweetable Quotes

Tweet the following quotes with these hashtags: #allinthesameboat #eliminatefailureasanoption

"Every submarine sailor knows there are no other options; you must reach the surface."

"Create a culture that attacks problems with the same attitude and tenacity as a submarine crew trying to reach the surface."

"Building a mindset, culture, and systems that can consistently achieve targets regardless of the challenges is powerful."

"Any leader can achieve consistent performance; it just takes a mindset and a persistent, unwavering commitment to reinforce non-negotiable goals."

"Deciding not to fail is a choice."

"It's one thing to say that failure is not an option. It's another to build the infrastructure to ensure failure never happens."

"Often, the fear of failure can motivate you to your absolute best performance."

Questions to Ponder

1. What are the non-negotiable goals in your organization?

2. What is the mindset required for meeting these goals?

3. How are you building a culture that is not willing to allow failure?

4. What systems and processes are in place to ensure continued flawless execution?

Chapter 5. Lead Like You Are All in the Same Boat

The global submariner community is a very special one. Long an elite cadre of highly skilled sailors and daring commanders, all submariners are aware of their shared vulnerability. Operating deep below the oceans, survival can never be taken for granted.

– Tom Rogan, foreign policy writer for the *Washington Examiner*

Countdown

The celebration of "halfway night" was a distant memory. We had traveled long and far from Kings Bay, but no longer. Every nautical mile we steamed now brought us closer to our families. Making turns for home is the most incredible feeling on a nuclear submarine. Sure, we were proud to do our jobs – but after nearly 50 days at sea, we were all ready to get home.

At this point in the patrol we were starting to run out of supplies. The fresh fruits and vegetables were long gone, and the cooks had replaced our milk with the powdered variety, which I could never get used to. Three-bean salad from a can was served at almost every meal at this point, and "bug juice," a sugary drink made from a mysterious powder, flowed freely in the crew's mess. Our supply officer was carefully monitoring our remaining coffee stores. The chief of the boat was checking the toilet paper inventory. We could not afford to run out of either one of these essential provisions.

In a long Navy tradition, the crew had carefully squirreled away all sorts of sodas, candy bars, snacks, cigarettes, and food from home. The longer we were at sea, the more valuable these items became. Bartering and trading were common. I went to sea with several cases of Mountain Dew hidden in my stateroom. I could trade a can of Mountain Dew for almost anything I needed, including a candy bar or even a haircut. Sailors who had talents like cutting hair, repairing uniforms, or fixing personal electronics could barter their skills for these valuable commodities.

I was standing watch as officer of the deck on a quiet Saturday afternoon when several crew members came up to control to talk to me. They wanted to know when I was making my signature "days to go" sign again. They sought me out because they knew I had a particular skill. I couldn't cut hair or fix circuit boards but I could draw. I was the ship's cartoonist (or at least I was the guy people came to when they needed a funny drawing of something). They knew I was responsible for creating and posting the now-famous "days to go" sign for the past five patrols, and it was nearly time for it to go up again.

I don't know if the tradition of posting this sign was widespread in the Navy or just something we did on the *Tennessee*, but it was a ritual I loved being involved with. The concept was straightforward. I would hand-draw and laminate a sign and display it in the missile compartment. At 24 days left on patrol, I would place it on missile tube #24 right above the large number "24" painted on the side of the tube. Each day I would move the sign to the next missile tube to count down our remaining days at sea.

What made it especially fun is that I would draw humorous images of the most memorable events that occurred on that patrol in a fashion similar to a *Where's Waldo?* drawing. There were so many details on the sign that officers and sailors alike would stop to take in all the particulars. It was a whimsical reminder of what we'd all been through for the past month and a half. It was also an important countdown to the future. The sign had a large arrow on the bottom of it, pointing to the missile tube number with a reminder of the most critical thing we all wanted to know: "Days to Go."

It didn't matter what your rank was, if you were qualified or not, or how many patrols you had made. We all looked forward to one thing – getting home. And unlike other military units where personnel rotated in and out of duty stations regularly, our crew remained the same. The team that had left port nearly 50 days ago was still here, and we all had just weeks to go. From beginning to end, we were in this together.

One thing that is unique in the tight, cramped quarters on a submarine that you don't see in other organizations is that nobody really had any special privileges. There was no special treatment for the officers and senior enlisted personnel. On board, everybody ate the same food, wore the same uniform (the famous blue poopy suit), and slept on the same size coffin-like rack. If we ran out of something, no one had it. When the freshwater supply was low, no one got showers. When the galley was secured for maintenance or drills, we ate cold cuts. Officers and sailors alike spent countless hours together standing six-hour watches in cramped spaces like control, sonar, radio, and maneuvering. When we ran drills, everybody participated, and when required, everyone sucked rubber. When one suffered, we all suffered. On a submarine at sea, there is no "us and them."

This tight-knit, shared work environment was unique even in the Navy. While I was stationed at Kings Bay, I remember visiting a friend on the aircraft carrier *USS Saratoga* down in Mayport, Florida. I couldn't get over how large the spaces were and all the amenities available to the crew. The one thing that really stood out during the tour was a sign I saw in a stairwell leading up to the officer's area of the ship. The sign read, "Make yourself presentable. You are entering Officer Country." There was even a mirror mounted on the wall so sailors could check their appearance before heading up. *What a joke*, I thought. There wasn't much of an officer country on the *Tennessee*, and we certainly didn't expect sailors to tidy up before they walked in. The truth is, on a submarine on patrol, none of us looked very presentable, including the officers. There may have been an element of "us and them" on aircraft carriers, but we didn't have room for that luxury on our boat.

On the *Tennessee*, we didn't eliminate the "us and them" mindset by design; it just happened. The tight environment didn't allow any crew members to have special privileges. On board, we shared things equally. We shared responsibility, vulnerability, suffering, failure, and success. We had to work as one team if we wanted to survive and return safely to our families. Each of us knew the enemy was outside the hull, and it wasn't just the Soviets. We operated alone, in the middle of the Atlantic, surrounded by an emotionless and indifferent adversary. There were thousands of pounds of sea pressure over our heads that wanted to crush us like a tin can and send us to the bottom of the ocean. We all knew if that happened, none of us would survive. We were all in it together. We were all in the same boat.

We also knew that no one was more important than another for our survival. We needed each other. It didn't matter what your rank was. Each of us had a unique and critical role to play in safely operating this $2 billion warship. Everyone would be affected if one sailor turned the wrong valve, if an officer gave the wrong order, or if the captain made the wrong decision. We depended on each other for our very lives. This interdependence was why getting qualified and earning dolphins was so important. You had to prove your worth before other crew members would trust you. But once that trust was earned and there were dolphins on your chest, there was mutual respect. You knew your shipmate had your back.

On a submarine crew, everyone is essential. My early experiences as a leader in the unique world of submarine operations established a foundation I have used in business for nearly 30 years. I have applied the simple concept of "all in the same boat" throughout my career. Like my Navy days, I have always sought to eliminate the "us and them" mentality in the organizations I've led and have tried to minimize any special privileges for managers – for example, assigned parking. I've also worked to eliminate internal politics by directing the organization's efforts to battle the enemies outside the four walls. Like the seawater surrounding the *Tennessee*, every business is encircled by "enemies" that don't want to see you succeed. Having a unified front and focusing efforts toward external enemies has helped keep internal politics at bay in the organizations I have led.

Finally, I believe every employee is essential to an organization's success. Each person plays a unique role in accomplishing the mission, and no one is better than anyone else. When taking over a business, the first thing I do is establish a culture of mutual respect, which begins with me. From the newest hire to the most senior employee, I treat everyone with respect. I also have zero tolerance for disrespect in the organization.

If you can't demonstrate respect for your coworkers, you don't have a place in my company. My message is clear: Everyone is vital to our success, and I expect you to have your coworker's back.

Operation Flying Fish

I took a short nap in the early morning hours after we finally surfaced but I was still exhausted. The past three days were a blur. I think I had slept a total of six hours during the past 72 hours. The good news is that the evaluation was complete, and we would soon be home. The bad news is I had the morning watch as officer of the deck. We were meeting tugs outside Port Canaveral at 1100 for the riders to depart. Everybody on board was glad to get these guys off our boat.

At the end of every patrol, the Navy tested us before we could go home to our families. We either had an Operational Reactor Safeguard Examination (ORSE) or a Tactical Readiness Evaluation (TRE). The ORSE tested our engineering department's readiness and ability to handle reactor emergencies. The TRE tested our overall war-fighting capabilities.

This time, it was the TRE. We ran drills and conducted battle scenarios for three days straight, and we were all drained. The senior naval officers sent to evaluate our performance had been especially tough this time. The lead officer, in particular, was a real stickler. He gave us low marks and forced us to repeat several drills for seemingly minor infractions. We had trained hard for this patrol and we were highly capable, but we couldn't seem to please this one inspector. It felt like he had a bias against our crew and was trying to make a statement.

His actions left our sleep-deprived crew frustrated, but I was proud of how everyone responded. Not once did I see any infighting or finger-pointing – just the opposite. Every time the TRE evaluators tried to get tougher on our crew, everyone on board just worked harder to prove them wrong. The crew saw the evaluators as outsiders, enemies, and something that had to be overcome and defeated. Eventually we ended up getting the high marks we deserved on the TRE but not without a lot of extra effort. The sooner we could get these guys off the boat, the better, and I couldn't wait until 1100.

As I climbed the long ladder of the conning tower up to the bridge to take over the watch, the pungent smell of the ocean instantly woke me up. After being submerged for more than 70 days, I was happy to be outside breathing fresh air again. The lookout watch had come up before me and scanned the horizon for surface ships while I began my turnover. After I assumed the watch as officer of the deck, the lookout pointed to the back of the boat and said, "Check that out." I glanced down at the flat back of the *Tennessee* and saw it right away. In stark contrast to the jet-black hull were dozens of silver flying fish lying dead on the deck.

Flying fish were common in this area. When we operated on

the surface, we could usually see them leaping from the ocean to avoid predators. Flying fish can "fly" up to 150 feet during their escape. It was not uncommon to find them scattered on the deck of the boat after we surfaced. A submarine on the surface causes them to panic, and they often ended up landing on the flat back of the boat. Usually the first sailors on deck would toss them overboard, but since we had been on a long surface transit this morning, no one had been on deck yet. So those fish just stayed there, rotting and stinking in the morning sun.

At 1030 we made contact with the tugs out of Canaveral and began steaming toward the rendezvous point. I gave the command to get the topside watch and the inspectors on deck for the transfer. I knew they would use the aft missile compartment hatch, so I quickly looked back to make sure my orders were being carried out. Several of our crew emerged first, carrying the inspectors' baggage. I watched as they placed the bags carefully on the deck. Assuming everything was in order, I resumed my focus on the tug operations. At 1100, the gangplank from the lead tug landed on the *Tennessee's* deck, and the riders departed without incident. They were gone, and we could finally make our way home to Kings Bay.

After turning over the watch, I headed down to the wardroom for lunch. Despite being tired, everyone was in a good mood. When I entered the wardroom, it was filled with roaring laughter. Something funny just happened, and I missed it.

"What's going on?" I asked.

One of the junior officers said, "I thought you knew." But I had no idea. He smiled, "It happened on your watch."

He proceeded to tell me what happened topside while I was busy coordinating with the tugboats. Several of the officers and sailors had "taken revenge" on the TRE evaluators. While the inspectors' baggage was topside and the inspectors were still below, our crew took the liberty of filling each bag with dead and decaying flying fish.

"And that's not the best part," one of the other officers said. "I took the dirty pair of underwear I've been wearing for the past three days and put it in the lead inspector's bag."

In my sleep-deprived state, I thought this was the funniest thing I had ever heard, and I joined in the boisterous laughter.

I learned a valuable lesson that week about being on a unified team. We all saw the TRE inspectors as outsiders. The stress of being tested didn't create internal conflict among the crew; it brought us together. Everyone worked in unison to "defeat" a common enemy, even so far as adding an extra dose of dead flying fish for effect.

In business, especially in large corporations, it's rare to find a unified team. It's more common to see internal conflict where the enemy is a rival department. Hearing comments like "It's marketing's fault" or "Engineering didn't do their job" are far too commonplace. But it's the role of the leader to address this. The leader is responsible for building unity and directing employees' frustrations toward the real adversary –

the competition. This is what it means to lead like you are all in the same boat.

Entry-Level Position

On my first deployment, I was a NUB, and I knew it. I was in that uncomfortable place of being deployed on a submarine and being unqualified. I was breathing the air and eating the food, but my shipmates couldn't depend on me in an emergency. Like every other officer and sailor who had come before me, I wanted to become an asset, not a liability. I wanted to do something valuable. The desire to add value helped me find and complete my first qualified position early in my first patrol. It wasn't the stately position of officer of the deck; it was a lowly entry-level position, yet still critically important to our mission.

At this point in my naval career, I was an ensign. I wore a single gold bar on my collar, which gave me the envious nickname of "butter bar" amongst the other officers. An ensign is equivalent to a second lieutenant in the Army, Air Force, and Marines. As you can imagine, the butter bar gets the assignments no one else wants. In my case, I didn't care. I just wanted to do something valuable, something to help the crew. After asking what roles I could fill as a NUB ensign, I found out about the battery charging lineup officer. This position was neither exciting nor glamourous. It was grunt work, but vitally important grunt work, and I was up for anything.

The job involved walking through the entire boat and verifying the ventilation system was ready to properly ventilate the battery compartment during a battery charge. It also involved entering the tight quarters of the battery compartment and checking the condition of the large 126-cell lead-acid battery. It was a vitally important job where one mistake could spell disaster. During the battery charging process, dangerous hydrogen gasses are formed that must be ventilated. An increased concentration of hydrogen gas can lead to a fire or an explosion, as it did for the *USS Pomodon* in 1955.

On February 21, while charging her batteries at the San Francisco Naval Yard, the *Pomodon* experienced a dangerous build-up of hydrogen gas, which caused a series of explosions and a fire. Five sailors were killed, and the boat was heavily damaged in the blaze. This incident and others like it are why the Navy takes battery charging very seriously. It's also why they required an officer (albeit very junior) to verify conditions are set up correctly for a battery charge.

When I learned I could qualify as the battery charging lineup officer as a junior officer, I jumped at the opportunity. It was my first chance to become an asset to the crew. I understood it meant waking up in the middle of the night, crawling into tight spaces, and getting acid burns on my clothing, but I couldn't wait to get started. The current battery charging lineup officer was more than happy to give up the job.

He had been the butter bar on the last patrol. He gladly answered all my questions and guided me through the qualification process.

In short order I finished my qualifications and became the battery charging lineup officer for that deployment. I was now doing something to add value to the crew. They could count on me to do my job to keep everyone safe during this dangerous procedure. As I think about that patrol, I have fond memories of being alone in the battery compartment in the middle of the night performing a task I knew was critically important. I remember the pungent smell of battery acid and the challenge of operating the hydrometer in the dim light and the slow roll of the boat.

Moreover, I remember the sense of pride I felt finally being an asset. I also saw the crew's attitude change when they saw me crawling through the ship and checking the position of valves with my trusty Maglite. I was young and inexperienced, but I was now qualified to do something meaningful. In a way, they were entrusting their lives to me.

The lesson I learned on that patrol was that every member of the crew is essential. We just had different jobs. Even though I wasn't qualified to stand watch as officer of the deck, I could still add value to the crew. In the middle of the night, while others slept, I quietly and competently did my job and kept my shipmates safe. This lesson always stuck with me. We all had a job to do, from the lowest seaman pulling crank duty on the mess decks to the commanding officer writing the night orders. We were all critical to the safe and effective operation of the *Tennessee*.

Sadly, the view that every employee is essential was not something I saw a lot of in the 22 years I worked in corporate America. Many managers didn't see things as I did. There wasn't a universal appreciation for workers who quietly took care of business day in and day out for years on end, especially manufacturing and call center employees. There was a prevailing attitude in upper management that those jobs weren't necessary and could just be outsourced or moved offshore.

These managers didn't see these jobs and the people who did them as critically important to the mission of the business. Unfortunately, many of these same managers saw themselves as more important to the company than the workers adding value on the shop floor or taking care of customers on the phone. It's no wonder why employee engagement in corporate America is so low.

The idea that every employee is vital to the organization regardless of his or her position is powerful. When you realize that every team member is critical, you have a different attitude towards even your most junior employee. In my case, I was the most junior officer on the boat, yet what I did was essential to the success of our mission.

We were "all in the same boat" on the *Tennessee*. That meant we were in it together. Every person was important, and we each had a critical role in carrying out our mission. When you have this mindset, you learn to appreciate every employee's contribution, regardless of rank or experience. When you demonstrate this behavior as a leader, you can create a culture of mutual respect throughout the team.

THE BUSINESS WORLD: FRIDAYS ON THE FLOOR

Every afternoon I would leave my office and wander around the shop floor. I was new to this business and new to manufacturing. I loved to get out and learn what was going on in the factory. Most of the longstanding employees enjoyed talking with me and showing me what they were working on. I think they were a little surprised to see the plant manager out on the floor so much, but it was clear they were proud of their jobs and eager to show me what they were doing.

When I first started making my rounds, I was overwhelmed with all the people, equipment, sights, sounds, and even smells in the plant. A manufacturing plant in full production is a sensory overload. I was also a bit self-conscious. I knew I was the youngest plant manager this operation had ever seen. I was inexperienced at just 32 years old and only five years out of the Navy. If I wanted to lead this plant well, I needed to learn from the more experienced employees, so I spent the afternoons observing and talking to people. I also watched how they made the components and built the products. The more time I spent in the plant, the more I started to see.

One afternoon I was walking by one of the stations where parts were brought together and built into various subassemblies. I noticed an employee using an unusual rubber mallet to connect the tight-fitting components. Using a mallet was standard practice, but what wasn't standard was the mallet itself. It didn't look like any I had ever seen. It was so worn down by extended use that the ends of the mallet didn't extend much past the handle. I needed to understand what was going on, so I stopped and talked to the operator.

Pointing to the mallet, I asked, "Is that normal?"

He just laughed and said, "No. Not really."

He proceeded to tell me that many of the hand tools on the line were old and worn down. He brought out a few examples to show me. I saw a bench full of worn-out wrenches, punches with mushroomed tips, and screwdrivers with missing handles; I was shocked.

"Why haven't you asked for replacements?" I asked with genuine curiosity.

His answer surprised me as he smiled and said, "Honestly, we're making do with what we have. We didn't want to bother management with something so trivial."

I immediately asked him for a list of tools he needed on the line to order replacements, but this experience bothered me. While I appreciated the desire of experienced employees to persevere despite the circumstances, I kept thinking, *How widespread is this problem? How is this affecting our overall performance? What other things are wrong in the plant that employees are not telling management?* However, the real question I was struggling with was a simple one: *How do I get employees and management to communicate better?*

The biggest problem, I thought, was the "us and them" environment that existed in the plant. I noticed there was even a physical separation between the two main groups of employees at this operation. The white-collar workers, like marketing, accounting, engineers, and managers, all worked in two office areas on each side of the plant. The blue-collar workers all worked on the shop floor. While each group shared break areas and restrooms, there were very few shared experiences between the groups. The office team worked in the office, and the manufacturing team worked in the plant.

As I thought back to my days in the Navy, I realized how different this environment was from what I experienced on the sub. In the *Tennessee's* tight confines, there were very few areas of the boat where officers and enlisted worked separately. It was just the opposite. On patrol, officers and sailors spent days standing watch together. We knew each other very well because we talked for hours on watch. We shared every experience together – the endless, boring midwatches, as well as the battle station watches where we fired missiles and torpedoes for proficiency. There was no physical separation between the two groups on the boat. We worked together as one unit, each with different roles. If there was a problem, we all knew about it, and we worked together to fix it.

The challenge was trying to replicate something like this in the factory. Here the roles were clearly defined and had been rigidly adhered to for years. The office team worked in the office, and the manufacturing team worked in the plant. This is the way things were. But I kept thinking there was a better way. I thought, *What would happen if we changed things up?*

My idea started small. I knew the best thing we could do to build shared experiences was to work together. I also knew it needed to begin with me, so I started working on the shop floor. On the first Friday of every month I worked in a different factory area for four hours before lunch. Factory employees would teach me how to do the job, and I would work with them throughout the morning. Through this process I got to know the employees better, they got to know me, and I learned more about where our problems were. For the first time, management and factory workers worked together, sharing an experience and learning together.

If you think about it, having the plant manager working on the shop floor was a lot like the TV show *Undercover Boss*, but I was doing it 10 years before the show aired and I wasn't undercover. If you have ever seen the show, the lessons are powerful. Each episode features a senior manager at a major business going undercover as an entry-level employee to discover how the company really works. The senior manager works with the lowest-level employees at the company and sees it from their perspective. In the process, managers get to know the employees and discover many problems they didn't even know existed. Through this shared experience, problems that were once hidden are revealed to management.

Every month, after my shop-floor sessions, I would gather the plant management team and tell them what I had learned. They could tell I was excited. I would discuss everything that needed to be addressed on the line. I felt like I had just been given all the answers to the test we are all taking. I had uncovered so many hidden problems in the operation that I became obsessed with addressing all of them. It only took a few monthly sessions like this to realize that the management team didn't share my enthusiasm. They were respectful because I was the boss, but they didn't share my excitement. And it didn't take me long to realize why.

The answer was simple. The management team didn't have the same shared experience as I did. They were listening to me describe challenges they had never seen themselves. I knew right away that if I wanted to really bridge the gap between "us and them," more managers needed to see what I was seeing. More managers needed to get out of their offices and work directly with shop employees. That's when I decided to implement a new program at this business called "Fridays on the Floor."

On the first Friday of every month, all managers would work on the shop floor for four hours in the morning. Every manager had to keep notes of everything they learned on the line. At the end of these morning sessions, I would bring in lunch and gather the management team to see what everyone learned and what actions we needed to take. The end result of getting everyone involved was precisely what I expected. The managers were as excited as I was. They had uncovered dozens of problems that had gone unanswered for years. Outdated procedures, worn-out tooling, training deficiencies, quality problems, and hidden rework were just some of the issues found through these sessions.

More importantly, we began bridging the gap between management and the workers. The production employees were excited that management was finally paying attention and trying to make conditions better. A common understanding of the challenges in the plant began to evolve. Managers got to know shop employees better, and deeper relationships were formed. When managers realized how difficult some of the production processes were and how skilled the employees were, respect deepened. In the same fashion, shop employees learned what managers were doing in their offices each day. They realized how difficult their job was as well. Mutual respect spread throughout the operation.

Fridays on the Floor became standard practice at this operation, and it helped us build unity in the organization. As we broke down barriers between blue-collar and white-collar employees, we began to appreciate each other. As we worked together to fix the problems that were uncovered, our performance improved. Customers recognized our improved performance with even more orders. In the end, this manufacturing business was incredibly successful because of one worn-out mallet.

The lesson of Fridays on the Floor is summed up in a phrase we used in the Navy: "Expect what you inspect." In every organization, you will find managers who think they understand the challenges facing their business. However, most of that understanding is built mostly on assumptions. Without spending time where the value is added (in our case, the shop floor) and without getting to know the people directly involved with the process, there is no way to know for sure. Most management teams have no idea what's going on in their business because they rarely leave their offices. It's only when you work together, break down the barriers between "us and them," and truly build shared experiences that you really understand the challenges.

I also learned that spending time together built mutual respect and a common understanding of the difficulties in the business. Instead of pointing the finger towards workers and blaming them for productivity numbers, managers now understood the challenges employees faced. Instead of wondering what managers did all day, the workers saw management actively involved in solving problems. The shared work experience of Fridays on the Floor built unity in our business. It helped break down barriers, eliminated internal politics, and focused our efforts on common problems.

LAST WATCH

"What are you working on, Mr. Rennie?" The voice startled me. It was the messenger of the watch. I was quietly working in my stateroom while the other officers slept. The messenger was a young sailor making the rounds to ensure each of the watchstanders was up and ready to take over the next watch.

"Do you promise not to say anything?" I asked. He nodded and smiled. Every sailor liked a good secret. "I'm designing a pirate flag. I plan to fly it from the bridge on my last watch." His smile deepened.

About halfway through my last patrol on the *Tennessee*, I hatched a plan. I decided to do something special. I had spent more than 500 days of my life under the ocean and had fulfilled my life's dream of becoming a submariner. In just a few weeks it would all be over. I had informed my commanding officer that this patrol would be my last and I'd be leaving the Navy. As the days ticked by on my last voyage, feelings were bittersweet. It would be a sad day to walk off the *Tennessee's* gangplank for the last time, but I was excited for what the future had in store.

I wanted to make the most of my last watch. I had already arranged it with the captain to take the final officer of the deck watch before we went into port. That meant I would have the midwatch as we steamed on the surface toward the sea buoy just outside the Cumberland Sound entrance. The captain also agreed I could keep the American flag that flew over the *Tennessee* this patrol as a reminder of my time on board. The final part of my plan didn't have clearance from the captain and was a bit controversial. I planned to do something that submariners had been doing for decades. I would replace the American flag with a pirate flag for my final six hours as the watch officer.

"There is a touch of the pirate about every man who wears the dolphins badge." Those words were spoken by retired Royal Navy submarine commander, Jeff Tall. And he's right. In the early days of submarining, many naval traditionalists saw submarine warfare as inherently unfair and problematic. In 1900, British Admiral Arthur Wilson said that submarines were an "underhand form of attack" and that their crews should be "treated as pirates." As a result, submariners have always had a bit of a pirate mystique.

Among British and American submarine captains, there is a tradition of flying a pirate flag from the boat's bridge after successful patrols. This practice traces its roots back to World War I. Max Horton, who commanded the British submarine *HMS E9*, was thought to be the first to fly the iconic pirate flag. He raised the skull and crossbones upon returning to port after sinking the German battle cruiser *Hela* in 1914. Many think it was in direct response to Admiral Wilson's criticism.

This tradition spread to American submarines, especially those operating in the Pacific theater in World War II. American boats flew both the Jolly Roger and custom hand-sewn battle flags upon returning from successful war patrols. It was a practice I always found fascinating. It's hard to know precisely why I felt the need to hoist a pirate flag on my last watch, but I think it was a quiet nod to all the submarine sailors who had come before me. I chose this life because I was heavily influenced by the heroic stories of World War II submarine crews. Maybe it was just my way of giving a final salute to them on my last watch.

Despite my best efforts, word of my plan spread throughout the boat. It was hard to keep a secret on a submarine at sea. What was meant to be a quiet salute to past submariners was quickly becoming a team effort. As officers and sailors caught wind of what I was doing, they all wanted to help. One of the mess specialists gave me a white sheet to use for the flag's iconic skull and crossbones. The damage control assistant gave me a large piece of black cloth to be the central part of the flag. He had used the fabric to simulate smoke during fire drills on that patrol. One of the quartermasters gave me a length of white rope to use as the flag's backbone. Another sailor who repaired uniforms on the side even gave me some needles and black thread.

I spent the next several weeks cutting and hand-sewing a four-foot by three-foot pirate flag. I had never sewn before, and it showed. The flag was childish and crude but certainly reminiscent of the custom, hand-sewn battle flags of World War II. As I quietly worked on the flag in my stateroom, I thought about the sailors who had come before me and the men I was serving with today. I would undoubtedly miss these men and this life. When the flag was complete, I kept it carefully hidden. Even though many people knew what I was doing, I was worried that the captain would find out and stop me.

Days before my final watch I learned something else I wasn't expecting. A long line of sailors and officers had "signed up" to serve as the lookout watch while I was on the bridge for my last watch. Normally as officer of the deck, I would stand watch with just one lookout on the bridge. The lookout would typically rotate every two hours with another sailor to keep their eyes fresh. However, on my final watch, there would be a long line of my shipmates coming to the bridge. They wanted to see the flag, take pictures, reminisce, and enjoy a cigar with me on my last watch. I couldn't have been more excited to share this final experience with them.

On that last night I made my way up the long ladder to the bridge, knowing this was the last time I would ever make this climb. I had the pirate flag, a disposable camera, cigars, and a lighter carefully packed in my foul-weather jacket. It was a warm night but windy with a light drizzle. It wasn't the calm, star-filled night I was hoping for, but it would do. I was anxious to get the pirate flag flying and light my first cigar. I had somehow managed to keep this a secret from the captain, and there wasn't much he could do now. He had gone to bed early and would be unaware of the unusual activities taking place on this watch.

With help from the lookout watch, I replaced the American flag with my handmade Jolly Roger. As the black-and-white flag whipped in the wind and the rain stung my face, I took it all in. It was a dark night and I knew that no one outside of the crew would even know this was happening, but I did. I proudly watched the skull and crossbones struggle in the squall, and I considered my small place in the history books. I was just another submariner in a long line of submariners who had come before me. I knew there would be many more who would come after me as well. I sat back and lit my first cigar. I planned to enjoy the next six hours.

One by one, my shipmates made their way up to the bridge, officers and enlisted alike. It was a cramped space with only room for four of us at a time. We smoked cigars, took pictures, and laughed at old stories. We talked about people we knew from past patrols and wondered where they all were. There were a few sailors whom I had served with from the start. We had made seven patrols together. I laughed as they told stories of a younger version of me trying to figure out life as a submariner. That night was a celebration of the unique bonds and friendships we had formed in the *Tennessee's* tight spaces.

This was not just a crew; this was my family. These were my brothers. We had served side by side for the past four years together. We had deep love and respect for each other, and I cherished every moment of that night. After steaming for six hours on the surface, the circling gulls noisily announced our arrival at the sea buoy. My last watch as a submarine officer was over. As the eastern horizon was flooded with brilliant colors, the last of my shipmates headed down for breakfast. I gathered my flags, turned over the watch, and headed down as well. It was hard to believe my time in the Navy was coming to an end. I was filled with mixed emotions as I climbed down the ladder to control. I reported in to the chief of the watch: "Lieutenant Rennie, down from the bridge." He smiled, shook my hand, and said, "Congratulations, sir."

That night was a powerful reminder of the impact we make on other people and how that affects us as well. In 2013, the Dalai Lama famously said, "Just as ripples spread out when a single pebble is dropped into water, the actions of individuals can have far-reaching effects." I would argue that, inside the hull of the *Tennessee,* any positive ripples I ever created as a leader reflected back on me tenfold. When you lead like you are all in the same boat, you positively affect your team and, in turn, they provide a deep impact on your life as well.

The Business World: Building a Team

As I watched a group of employees pass the 60-year-old production technician through an opening in the ropes, I suddenly realized this could be a bad idea. *What if they drop her?* I thought. This was supposed to be fun. I wanted to create a common, shared experience and bring us all together, but I hadn't really considered the age and physical condition of my employees. I was young and full of crazy ideas, but I also understood how important this was. I watched as the employees on the other side carefully lifted the woman through the opening and set her on her feet on the other side. She laughed, cheered, and high-fived all her teammates. As they all hugged and celebrated, I smiled. *Maybe this wasn't so crazy after all.*

As plant manager, I had embarked on the largest team-building event this manufacturing operation had ever seen. When I first came up with the idea, the production manager thought I was nuts. Who takes 160 employees away from work for a day of team building in the woods? He was concerned with the cost and the loss of production, while all I cared about was changing the culture. In the past, the managers of this plant went off by themselves on a retreat or a team-building event. To me, that didn't make much sense. If we wanted to eliminate the "us and them" mindset, we had to involve the entire team.

The plan was to have five outings, each with around 30 employees. The goal was to create a shared experience to build unity as a team. I wanted to replicate what I learned on the *Tennessee*. I wanted to create a culture of mutual respect where every employee knew he or she was essential to our success. I also wanted to eliminate the prevailing internal conflict and replace it with a cohesive team who understood the enemy was outside the plant's four walls.

We chose a local company to host the events. They had a remote location in the woods with a ropes course and a lakeside cabin to conduct training. It was the perfect setting to get away from the factory and create a memorable experience. We would spend the morning on the ropes course, have a group lunch, and train in the afternoon.

The training session was designed to introduce employees to several new concepts. My HR manager and I were both certified in lean manufacturing, and we would be sharing this methodology with the employees. Lean manufacturing is a production philosophy popularized by the automotive manufacturer Toyota. It's designed to engage all employees in a relentless pursuit of eliminating waste in production processes.

We also planned to show a short film called *Gung Ho! Turn On the People in Any Organization*, which was based on a book by Ken Blanchard and Sheldon Bowles. This emotional film told the story of a fictitious manufacturing operation saved from closure by actively engaged employees working as a unified team. Both the training and film were designed to get employees thinking differently about their roles in operating the plant. If we were going to become a world-class manufacturing operation, I knew we needed every employee to be part of that collective effort.

The last session of the day was the most important. It was an open discussion of what was working in the plant and what wasn't. It was an opportunity for employees to think about what they had learned throughout the day and discuss how these ideas could be used to improve the operation. Having these sessions was critical. They allowed our employees to reflect on their experiences, internalize the message, and visualize their individual roles in the changes we were considering.

I attended all five of the off-site gatherings and was able to observe how each employee reacted to the day's activities. In the morning of every session, there was always apprehension. When they saw the ropes course for the first time, most employees were concerned. I could tell they were outside their comfort zone, and many questioned my judgment as a leader. Some even voiced their opinions to their coworkers. Most of the comments I overheard were things like "What are we doing here?" and "This seems like a waste of time."

As the events of the day took place, however, I noticed a change. There was a certain energy in the woods. It started small but grew throughout the morning. As employees overcame the challenges of the ropes course, they became excited. There were smiles, laughter, and an overall feeling of achievement. They were beginning to enjoy each event and were increasingly motivated to conquer the next obstacle. As I watched them work as a team and cheer each other on, I knew this was the start of something special.

That energy continued throughout the day. While we enjoyed a group lunch, I noticed employees were laughing and smiling as they recalled the morning's events. I had never seen the workforce interacting like this before, and I could almost see the bonds forming in real time. The joking, teasing, and laughter reminded me of my time in the Navy. On the *Tennessee* we were all in it together. We had each other's back, and we understood that every sailor was essential to our success. I was starting to see that being formed here as well.

The enthusiasm continued in the afternoon training sessions. Employees were actively engaged and quick to ask questions during the lean manufacturing presentation. They were also visibly moved by the *Gung Ho!* film. In stark contrast to their apprehension in the morning, I could tell no one thought this day was a waste of time. They saw management cared enough to involve all employees and invest in everyone. The message was clear: Every employee was critical to our success.

The real reward came at the end of the day, though. The final sessions to discuss how to implement what we had learned in the woods were powerful. They were a chance for employees to share their thoughts and, to my surprise, they weren't quiet. Everyone was actively engaged. They had strong opinions and wanted their voices heard. The discussions were positive, and any criticism was minor and purely constructive. I was glad to see there wasn't a lot of griping or complaining. Instead, employees were genuinely focused on solutions. They wanted to get better and fix the problems we had at the plant. They understood it was about working as a unified team to overcome challenges, just like on the ropes course. We had a common goal to make the business better, and we filled dozens of flip charts with ideas on how to move forward.

As plant manager, I noticed the attitude back at the factory changed almost overnight. There was less animosity between departments and more focus on solutions. There was less finger-pointing as well and more problem-solving. Employees were also more vocal. When they saw a problem, they made management aware of the issue, and they worked together to overcome the challenge. I was beginning to see a change in our culture.

I also noticed employees were much more engaged. In monthly all-employee meetings, for example, they asked a lot more questions. They were interested in how we were doing and if we were getting better. They wanted to know if we were reaching our targets. Instead of machine operators, assemblers, or shipping clerks, employees saw themselves as key players on a bigger team. They felt they were doing worthwhile work that had an impact on our overall performance as a company.

As a result of the increased employee engagement, our business results improved. All the things we measured – from quality to cost, delivery, and safety – got better. Within six months, our performance began to exceed our targets consistently. In just 18 months, we became the best-performing manufacturing plant in our division. We set new records for orders, revenues, and profits; but more importantly, we began feeling like a team. Employees sensed they were part of something special.

As upper management took notice of our efforts, they recognized us with various accolades and awards. They also transferred more product lines to our plant because of our reputation. As a result, the business continued to grow. In my third year leading the plant, our operation was nominated for the Manufacturer of the Year Award for the state of South Carolina. Although we finished second in the competition, there was a still sense of pride throughout the plant for even being considered.

Shortly after the award announcement, I received an unexpected letter from the CEO of a global company headquartered near our plant. He had heard the news of the remarkable turnaround in our operation's performance and the high level of employee engagement we had achieved. He congratulated me and, to my shock, offered me a role as a division vice president responsible for two large manufacturing operations in the Northeast. It was an incredible offer, one that would catapult my career, but I was torn. This was my first plant and I loved these employees. I had never thought about leaving, but this opportunity was significant. After declining the offer on two separate occasions, I eventually accepted it. It was the hardest decision I ever made in my career. Even harder was breaking the news to my employees. I was so proud of everything they had accomplished and how far we had come. It was sad knowing I would soon be leaving them.

I received many going-away gifts from the employees at this plant, but there is one that is my most treasured keepsake. It has been on the wall of every office I've had for the past 20 years. It's a framed photograph of all the employees standing in front of that plant. On the mat surrounding the picture are signatures from 160 of the best employees any leader has had the opportunity to lead. Written in bold letters on the top of the mat are three words we learned together during those impactful five days in the woods. They said goodbye in a way they knew would have a deep, personal meaning to me. Three short words that always take me back to those employees and the great things they accomplished: *Gung Ho, Friend!*

Leading like you are all in the same boat is all about building unity. It's about eliminating the "us and them" internal conflict that exists in most organizations. When employees understand that everyone is essential to the success of the business, you start to build a culture of mutual respect. For this plant, those five days in the woods gave us a shared experience that we used as a foundation to rebuild our culture. It helped us understand the importance of working together to overcome obstacles. That understanding followed us into the factory and deeply affected everything we did. Not only did our performance improve, but we also created a better working environment for everyone.

The Bottom Line

Key Points

- All in the same boat means eliminating the "us and them" mentality.
- Unified teams know the enemy is outside the four walls.
- Everyone is important in the organization; we just have different roles to play.
- Build unity by eliminating special privileges for certain groups of employees.
- Your most junior employee is essential to your mission.
- Learn to appreciate the importance of every employee, regardless of rank or experience.
- Shared experiences create mutual understanding.

Tweetable Quotes

Tweet the following quotes with this hashtag: #allinthesameboat

"All submariners are aware of their shared vulnerability and their shared responsibility. On a submarine crew, everyone is important."

"When you are all in the same boat, the enemy is outside the four walls, not inside."

"It's the role of the leader to create a unified team and to direct the frustrations of employees outward toward the true enemy – the competition."

"In corporate America, there is little appreciation for workers who take care of business day in and day out for years on end."

"Leaders create a culture of mutual respect by how they treat their most junior employees."

"Spending time where the value is added is the only way to truly understand what is going on in your organization."

"When you lead like you are all in the same boat, you positively affect your team and, in turn, they provide a deep impact on your life as well."

Questions to Ponder

1. What conditions exist that foster an "us and them" mentality in your organization?

2. What can be done to build shared experiences and eliminate the "us and them" mindset?

3. Define the enemy outside your four walls. What are you doing to make sure employees know what or who that is?

4. Think of your most junior employee. How does his or her role ensure the success of your company? Knowing this, how can you build a culture of mutual respect with all your employees?

Chapter 6. Develop a "No Escape" Mindset

He watched the brass gauges about and the iron men at the crank as he recalled H. L. Hunley saying his craft was but a "peripatetic coffin" under the waves. A whaler, a sailor, and now a seaman three times over, the captain – who had not spent as many years ashore – then gave the order to dive.

– Roman McClay, Author of *Sanction*, personal communication

Crime of the Century

"Man battle stations torpedo," came over the 1MC followed by the loud *bong-bong-bong* of the general alarm. "Man battle station torpedo," the command was repeated. The words echoed through engine room upper level.

"Seriously?" I said to the chief machinist's mate. "We weren't supposed to be having any more drills today."

The chief just smiled and said, "Never a dull moment on the *Tennessee*."

I was as about as far away as I could be from my battle station. I was the geoplot operator in the control room when we were engaging an enemy with torpedoes. Control was near the bow and I was all the way back in the engine room near the stern. I set off in a sprint. Manning battle stations was always a bit of controlled chaos. Everyone knew where they were supposed to be, but we all had to get there in the crowded and cramped hallways of the boat.

I made my way through the engine room into the missile compartment. I passed by one of my fellow officers on the way.

"What's going on?" he yelled.

"I have no clue," I yelled back as I raced by him and continued forward.

I passed several sailors who looked like they had just woken up. They groggily made their way to their assigned stations with a dazed look in their eyes, trying to wake up as they ran. I smiled because I had been there more times than I could count. There's nothing like being rousted from a deep sleep to the sounds of the general alarm. This was just a normal thing for a submariner.

I made it to control and set up the geoplot for battle stations. That meant moving all the charts out of the way and laying down a large sheet of blank white paper over the chart table. During battle stations torpedo, all we cared about was us and the enemy. The white paper is where I would make sense out of all the data that was coming into control. In a way, I was like an interpreter. Everyone depended on me to translate the information, make sense of what was happening, and provide recommendations. I loved this job and I was good at it.

Like all the other officers in control except the captain, I donned my sound-powered headphones so I could communicate with all the other watchstanders. I was hoping we wouldn't be here long. I still had work to do in the engine room. The sound-powered phones were rough on the ears too, especially when we were at battle stations for prolonged periods of time. They were a cumbersome but effective way to quietly communicate when things got heated during battle stations.

I heard chatter as I put on my headset. Everyone was wondering what was going on. No one knew.

The captain received reports from throughout the boat. In short order, the word came back to control that the ship was manned and ready for battle stations. Everyone in control quietly turned to look at the captain as he reached for the 1MC microphone. We were about to discover why we were here.

"Attention. This is the captain. It has come to my attention that someone has stolen a Walkman from another sailor," he said. I looked around the control room and saw the disbelief on everyone's faces. I felt reassured knowing I wasn't the only one who didn't understand how this statement related to the fact we were at battle stations. The captain continued, "We will remain at battle stations until the Walkman is returned to the chief of the boat. That is all."

"What in the actual f***?" was the first thing I heard from an unknown whisper over my headset which was followed by quiet laughter. After a long moment of silence, another whisper said, "What kind of moron steals something on a submarine?" Again, laughter. After several minutes a quiet voice imitating a Scooby-Doo villain said, "And I would have gotten away with it too, if it weren't for you meddling kids." At that point, we were having trouble containing ourselves. The laughter got a little louder and the captain caught wind of what was happening. His own officers weren't taking this seriously.

The captain addressed all of us in control. "Do you think this is funny?" The laughter died immediately as we all simultaneously decided to stare at our Navy-issued blue Sperry Top-Sider sneakers. "You think I'm kidding? I'm prepared to stay at battle stations for the rest of the day until the Walkman is returned." And we all knew he was serious.

About three hours into battle stations with no end in sight and nursing a splitting headache, I began to hear whispers over the sound-powered phones that something was happening. Rumor was that the thief had actually brought the stolen Walkman to the chief of the boat. After a few minutes, I looked up and saw the chief of the boat in control talking to the captain, who then reached up for the 1MC microphone. *This might finally be over*, I thought. In a booming voice, the captain informed the crew, "The Walkman has been returned. The sailor who stole it will be dealt with. Let this be a lesson that there will be no stealing on the *Tennessee* so long as I'm captain. Secure from battle stations."

After downing some ibuprofen in my stateroom, I headed back to the engine room to finish my work. I couldn't stop thinking about this incident, though. What did this sailor think was going to happen? He attempted to pull off what is likely the stupidest crime of the century. Didn't he understand there was no place to run to and nowhere to hide on a submarine at sea? Didn't he know he couldn't escape the consequences of his actions either? Needless to say, the offending sailor spent much of the remaining patrol working as a mess crank in the ship's galley.

On a submarine at sea there is no escape from the consequences of your bad behavior, and on patrol there is no escape from a bad colleague either. We left port with 15 officers and 140 sailors. And unless someone had to be airlifted off the boat for an illness or family emergency, we would return to port with 15 officers and 140 enlisted sailors. Like it or not, we were stuck with the crew we deployed with. We were trapped with people we liked and those we couldn't stand. And in this case, we couldn't avoid being around a sailor who was foolish enough to think he could steal a Walkman on a submerged submarine.

When people ask me what it's like to work on a nuclear submarine, I often tell them it's similar to going to work and one day having your boss lock the doors and informing employees that no one is going home. Only on a submarine, the office is a lot smaller. On board, you are stuck in the tight confines of the pressure hull 24 hours a day, seven days a week with the same 155 people for almost three months. There was no escape from a bad colleague. And this condition actually creates an interesting dynamic.

If you think about it, in most work environments it's easy to escape from bad colleagues. You can ignore them, avoid them, tell them to leave you alone, or report them to HR if their behavior is extreme. As a leader, you can transfer or even fire bad employees to address workforce conflict. On a submarine at sea, you can't do any of this and, in a way, it's a good thing. Submariners develop a unique set of interpersonal skills. They learn how to get along with people they have differences with. They learn to compromise and find common ground. They develop a higher tolerance for people with different opinions and personality types. In a time when most people have forgotten how to get along with people they disagree with, this is a critical skill.

Thinking back, this unique work environment prepared me well for my roles in corporate America. I worked for three global companies, traveled the world, and worked with every type of personality you can think of. I was often around people I disagreed with but always worked to find common ground and win-win solutions. Most of the interpersonal conflicts I had to deal with as a leader were with people who were unable to resolve their differences. If more people had the opportunity to serve on a deployed submarine for three months, they would have a lot more tolerance for those with different opinions and beliefs.

When there is no escape from a bad colleague or even someone you disagree with, you find ways to work together. You look for common ground and solutions that work for both parties. When you can't avoid the conflict, you tend to confront it and work it out. We also learned not to let problems linger. When you are forced to spend long hours together in tight spaces, you learn to forgive and forget quickly as well.

Cross-Threaded

I was trying to keep my cool, but the longer the watch went on, the angrier I got. It was the midwatch and, as officer of the deck, I had a lot to get done before 0600. The captain had left a long list of actions that needed to be completed before the morning watch. We would be running a full set of drills in the morning. The captain's orders were clear: Complete all the actions, no exceptions. Most midwatches were quiet, but tonight I was struggling to keep up with all the activity. What made it worse was that the weapons officer (or "weps") had decided to conduct a series of preventative maintenance operations, which was slowing my progress.

Whoop-whoop, the sound-powered phone sang out above my head. I grabbed it off the cradle and said, "Conn, officer of the deck." I was annoyed. It was weps again.

"Officer of the deck, weps. I need you to stop moving water around the ship and keep a 0 degree bubble." It wasn't a question; it sounded more like an order. Theoretically, he outranked me. Even though we were both lieutenants, he was on his department head tour and I was still a junior officer on my first tour. But, as officer of the deck, I was responsible for the ship and I didn't really have to do anything other than the actions in captain's night orders. This new request meant I couldn't pump the tanks that needed to be emptied this watch.

"For how much longer?" I snapped. "I've got a lot to do tonight."

After a long pause, he said, "Maybe an hour...tops."

I didn't even respond. I slammed the phone back in its cradle which was louder than I expected and caused everyone in control to look in my direction. I was annoyed and I really didn't care. I came on watch thinking I would have a quiet six hours of making holes in the ocean and now I was struggling to complete the captain's night orders. It was all because the weapons officer decided to do maintenance on my watch. My anger intensified as I considered this.

After watching the seconds tick on the control room clock for about 45 minutes, I was frustrated and couldn't wait any longer. *Whoop-whoop-whoop-whoop*, I angrily rang up the weapons officer.

"Weps," he responded calmly.

"How much longer? I've got work to do!" I said.

His answer floored me. "We're still getting set up back here. We haven't started yet. Maybe an hour…tops."

This was turning into a disaster. There was no way I would be able to complete the captain's night-order actions at this pace. My anger intensified, and at this point I completely lost it.

If you've ever seen the movie *Christmas Vacation*, you would get a feel for what happened next. In the movie, Clark Griswold, played by Chevy Chase, is doing all he can to have a picture-perfect family Christmas…except everything goes hilariously wrong. He reaches a boiling point when he opens up his Christmas bonus check in front of his family only to discover it had been replaced with a one-year membership to the "Jelly of the Month" club. What follows is considered one of the most epic rants in Hollywood history.

What I said to the weapons officer over the sound-powered phone that night rivaled the famed Clark Griswold rant. I called him and his men every name in the book and even some that weren't in the book. I went on for two minutes straight and then slammed the phone back in the cradle so loud that they probably heard it in Moscow.

Everyone in control stared at me in disbelief. I don't think they had ever seen an officer dress down another officer like that before, especially one that technically outranked him. There was an eerie quiet in the room after my tirade and everyone worked in silence the rest of the watch. No one brought it up for fear I would unleash my fury on them as well.

Develop a "No Escape" Mindset

The second the phone hit the cradle, however, I knew I had overreacted. I felt bad immediately. I knew weps was just trying to do his job and I was trying to do mine. In the high-stress world of underwater operations, sometimes things got heated. I knew what I needed to do. After a morning drill set full of fires, flooding, reactor scrams, and battle stations, I went right to the weapons officer stateroom.

"Weps, I'm sorry. I kind of lost it last night," I said as I sat down next to him in the tiny room.

He laughed. "Kind of? That was some sort of a rant." He smiled and continued, "It was the longest string of insults and putdowns I've heard my entire life. It was amazing, inspiring, truly epic. A work of art. I was completely impressed. I actually had to look up a few of those words you called me."

I was surprised by his reaction. "You're not mad?" I said.

"Nah," he said. "Forgive and forget. Things like this happen all the time. We were both just trying to do our jobs."

That was the end of it. The weapons officer and I continued to be friends and worked closely with each other throughout the rest of that deployment.

An important lesson you learn living on a nuclear submarine is that in the tight spaces of a submarine you can't let problems linger and go unaddressed. In an office setting you might be able to spend weeks avoiding someone you are at odds with. You can likely escape having that awkward moment running into them in the hallway or the break room. At sea, however, you can't avoid anyone. There's no room for pent-up emotions because there is no room for anything. If you did something wrong or someone did something wrong to you, you learned to forgive and forget quickly.

In 22 years working in corporate America I learned that having a forgive-and-forget mindset was both rare and powerful. Not harboring bad feelings and knowing how to resolve conflicts allowed me to get along with a wide range of personality types in all different roles. I was able to get things done with people I liked and those I had deep differences with. The weapons officer had the right approach. Instead of being offended, he laughed the whole incident off. For him, it was like water rolling off a duck's back. It didn't bother him at all. As it turns out, having thick skin is also an important thing I learned on board.

Belt Trimming

Life was good as a qualified officer. Almost too good. As one of the more senior division officers on my seventh patrol, I was actually enjoying my time on board. We had so many qualified officers that I only stood one six-hour watch every 24 hours. The rest of the time I worked with my division in the missile compartment, I slept, I ate, I worked out, I read books, and I watched movies…a lot of movies. I was living large for the first time as a submariner.

Develop a "No Escape" Mindset

One of my fellow officers, Paul, was also living large – maybe a bit too large. With all the food, reduced stress, and minimal physical activity, he had been slowly gaining weight. On our seventh patrol together he decided he was finally going to get a handle on it. He was going to start dieting and exercising.

It might surprise you to learn we had a small gym on board. It was at the aft end of the missile compartment on the lower level. We had two treadmills, two stationary bikes, a rowing machine, and a universal weight machine. It wasn't much but it was enough to break a sweat and stay in shape. I enjoyed running on the treadmills. It was a great way to burn energy and it was a welcome distraction from the lingering thought that I was stuck in a 560-foot metal tube for next few months. I had to be careful not to get too distracted, though. Behind the treadmills was a wall of pipes, brackets, and valves. One wrong step and you would be thrown into a world of hurt. I was always aware of that risk and stayed vigilant.

Paul set his sights on losing the weight and getting back in shape. He had three months to focus his efforts and he was motivated to make it happen. The problem was that he let too many people know about it.

It has been said that if something bothers you, the last thing you want is to let a submariner know it. That's because submariners will test you. They will tease you. They are relentless smack talkers and world-class pranksters. This playful teasing, where every minor flaw is exploited, is done with the best of intentions. In the high-stress world of underwater operations, submariners acted more like a family. Every lighthearted insult said you were accepted and part of the team. It also served to see how sensitive you were. Your shipmates needed to know if you were tough or fragile. They wanted to know if you had their back when things got ugly. If you couldn't laugh at yourself, you'd make a terrible submariner.

One of our other fellow officers, Sam, was just the kind of guy you never showed weakness towards. Sam was the master of pranks and loved to tease his fellow shipmates. One of my favorite things he would do as officer of the deck was to provide colorful commentary on anyone coming into control who just got out of bed. You know the look – dazed eyes, bedhead hair, wrinkled clothing, and facial creases where the pillow once was. When the general alarm went off, everyone jumped out of their rack and raced toward their battle station. No one took the time to try to look good, and Sam made sure to point out every flaw.

He had a name for those pillow-induced facial creases. He called them "rack burns." When groggy sailors entered control with their hair all askew and lines on their faces, he would laugh and say, "Oh, man. Look at those rack burns!" He loved to say, "Dude, I don't think you're gonna make it" or "You're burning up! It's looking bad." Most sailors would just laugh and go about their business. They knew he was a jokester. He threw insults my way on countless occasions and I always thought it was hilarious. Sometimes I would purposely mess up my hair just to see what he would say. There were a few guys who gave him a dirty look and took offense, but that never ended well. Showing weakness only increased his commentary.

Sam heard about Paul's weight-loss goal and hatched a plan. He was going to trim his uniform belt. Belt trimming is a common prank in the military. It involves trimming an eighth of an inch or so from the belt every few days. There was a metal end and an unfinished end on our webbed belts. The unfinished end was clipped behind the buckle. Secretly trimming the unfinished end and re-clipping it behind the buckle essentially reduced the length of the belt without the owner ever knowing it happened. The victim was left to think he was gaining weight.

All of the junior officers were in on Sam's prank. Everyone knew he was doing this. Any time Paul was in the shower, his belt and uniform were left hanging in his stateroom unprotected. The other officers would quietly inform Sam so he could sneak in and trim Paul's belt. This went on for weeks. As Paul lost weight, Sam continued to trim his belt, and we all patiently waited for Paul to say something.

One day it finally happened – Sam's trimming got a little too far ahead of Paul's weight loss. I was with Sam and several other junior officers in the officer's study when Paul walked in. His belt was especially tight around his waist and Sam couldn't hold back any longer.

Sam said, "I thought you were trying to lose weight, Paul."

Paul responded, "I am. I've lost 15 pounds so far."

Without a beat, Sam asked, "Then why is your belt so tight?"

Those of us who were in on the prank couldn't hold back. We all burst out in laughter, and as soon as the laughter started, Paul knew he had been pranked. He had been secretly wondering why his waist wasn't shrinking. He laughed along with us and finally asked who was responsible. He wasn't surprised when he learned it had been Sam trimming his belt all along. Paul took the prank in stride and thought it was just as funny as the rest of us. He was a great officer who didn't take himself too seriously, which is why we all loved serving with him.

Another great example of Paul's ability to laugh at himself came later in that patrol. Paul had added exercise to his daily routine and was regularly going to the missile compartment gym to get fit. One day didn't go very well. I was in the wardroom having lunch with several officers when Paul walked in. His sleeves were rolled up as well as the pants on his poopy suit. His arms and legs were covered in bandages. He looked like he just came off a battlefield.

We were all shocked. I was the first to ask him what happened. Paul smiled and said, "The treadmill ate me." He explained that he got distracted on the treadmill and lost his balance. He was thrown into the wall of pipes and valves behind the treadmill. While the treadmill was still running, he landed with his arms and legs on the treadmill deck, which proceeded to tear away his skin like a belt sander. We were all shocked and immediately felt bad for Paul – all of us except Sam.

In typical Sam fashion, he said in his best radio announcer voice, "The final score. Treadmill 1. Paul 0."

We all laughed out loud including Paul, who laughed the loudest.

Taking your job seriously but not yourself was an important lesson I learned on the *Tennessee*. I learned to laugh at myself and I grew thicker skin. I learned not to let little things bother me. Like water off a duck's back, I learned to not let insults, embarrassments, and shortcomings affect me. I learned to laugh at my failures and not take myself too seriously. As it turned out, this was perfect training for entering the corporate world.

The Business World: Swimming with Sharks

"They're screwing us, and you have to do something about it."

That was the report I just received from my new operations manager. I had just taken over another business in our division and was reviewing the financial numbers. I had discovered we were selling a product to another business inside our division at a loss. Margins were strong in this business except for one product line, and I was trying to understand why.

"Past management put a transfer price agreement in place that is unfair to us. You have to change that." The operations manager was clearly trying to put this monkey on my back.

I was one of ten vice presidents working for a division senior vice president. Five of us were operating the businesses and the other five were supporting the division with staff functions such as HR, purchasing, marketing, sales, and product management. We were all sharks. Each of the five businesses was a separate operating unit with its own profit goals. Each of the five operational vice presidents was doing his best to optimize his business, often at the expense of other businesses in the division. What's worse was that no one was stepping in stop this from happening. The senior vice president didn't have the time or energy to resolve petty differences. So the infighting continued, and it was intense at times.

The vice president of the business we had a transfer price problem with was a gruff, older, hardened executive. He had been in the industry for decades and was a man of few words. He was a tall, no-nonsense leader who had worked hard to turn his business around. He was known to be a tough negotiator, and I knew confronting him on this topic would be difficult. He wasn't the type who would give in to the demands of a younger executive like me, especially when my request would only serve to lower his profits.

I didn't have a bad relationship with him. We were friendly but I didn't know much about his background. I assumed he didn't care much for me. I had an undeserved reputation in the division of being the "golden child." The businesses I ran always did well, and we got results. We made our numbers. As a result, I received more than my share of attention, awards, and recognition, which made the other vice presidents jealous. They thought I was somehow getting special treatment. The truth was that I had successfully tapped into the collective wisdom of my teams. My employees were making things happen, but as the business leader, I received a lot of the credit… and some of my peers didn't like that at all.

I knew I couldn't go to my boss to resolve this transfer price problem. He stayed out of interdivisional spats. I would have to confront my peer directly, and I knew it wouldn't be easy. Employees in both businesses were well aware of this issue. It had been going for years. The battle lines were drawn. Employees in my business thought it wasn't fair that we were losing money selling our product to a sister business in the division. They felt we were "subsidizing" that business.

Employees in the other business felt they needed the lower price so they could be competitive with "real" customers. Many felt our business was far too profitable already, and they incorrectly assumed we were making all our money off internal customers. Any change to this transfer price policy would be seen as a win for one business and a loss for the other.

Fortunately for me, my experiences in the Navy prepared me well for this situation. I knew how to get along with people I had differences with. I knew how to compromise and find common ground, and I also had a high tolerance for people with different opinions and personality types. My colleague probably didn't like me but that didn't bother me at all. I was confident I could find a solution end to this bitter cold war between our two businesses.

We didn't make a lot of progress in our first meeting. We both presented our positions. He made it clear to me that he needed the lower price to be competitive and pointed out that my company was already making a sizable profit. In his mind, the current transfer price policy made sense. I made it clear that my company's profit came from sales of other products to external customers and that it wasn't fair for us to sell below our costs, especially since each business was measured on meeting our profit budgets. We both had excellent points and defendable positions. While neither of us gave any ground that first meeting, we both developed a better understanding of each other's positions.

We also found we had a lot in common. We both grew up in blue-collar families and had a passion for shop floor workers. We both had studied lean manufacturing and were pushing those best practices into our businesses. We each had spent years in operations management. We were both "plant rats" – guys in the back-office world of manufacturing who made their living working outside the limelight. I gained respect for him as I learned about all of the operations he had led in three different global companies. He learned that, while young, I also had led many manufacturing plants. It turned out we were more alike than we were different. At the end of our first meeting, I think he saw me as a younger version of himself. I wasn't a golden child at all. I was just another hard-working leader who was doing my best to run a successful manufacturing business.

After our first meeting, I understood his position, and it made sense. His competitors didn't have a problem with "margin stacking" like we had at our company. Their divisions worked as one large operating unit. Products transferred internally at cost, not marked up. My colleague would be at a competitive disadvantage if I sold my products to him at a profit.

In our next meeting, I made a proposal. I suggested we transfer product from our company to his company at cost. His business would not be at a competitive disadvantage and I wouldn't be losing money on this product. It was a compromise that had promise. It wasn't a perfect solution but it would give each of our teams a "win." I was shocked when I learned he was considering the same thing. He felt it wasn't right for us to sell below our costs either. In just two meetings we arrived at a compromise.

After that second meeting, we wrote up a new transfer pricing agreement that we both signed. We each went back to our teams and explained the changes. While neither side could claim a major victory, no one really lost ground either. We had resolved a long standing issue that had created animosity between our two teams. More importantly, this experience brought us closer together. We became friends. From that point on, we both looked out for each other. We had each other's back. If he heard about anything that could hurt my business or me personally, he would let me know. I did the same. We became allies – two sharks operating together as a team.

What I learned on the *Tennessee* I practiced countless times in the corporate world. On board there was no escape from someone you had a dispute with; you had to find ways to work together. You had to find common ground. You couldn't avoid the person or the conflict, so I learned to confront it and work it out. We didn't let problems linger on the submarine, and I never did in my corporate life either. I always tried to work things out even when someone did something against me personally. Resolving conflicts, finding common ground, and having a forgive-and-forget mindset – these were all principles that helped me become a more effective leader in the Navy and in the business world. I also learned to appreciate the unique personalities of my employees, because on deployment there was no escape from some of the most interesting characters.

McKinley

I was still trying to wake up. I had morning duty as engineering officer of the watch, and I made my way back to the engine room with a steaming mug of hot black coffee. I was hoping the dark liquid would give me the boost I needed to get through the next six hours. I slipped through the engine room hatch without spilling a drop and stopped to talk to the team in maneuvering. I told them I was going to conduct my pre-watch checks of the engine room before coming back to take over the watch.

We were trained to do a thorough walk-through of the engine room to make sure we understood the condition of the plant before we took over. I looked for valve leaks, checked tank temperatures, and verified the positions of switches and indicators. We were taught to use all our senses. I looked, listened, and even smelled for unusual conditions that could create a problem. I used the back of my hand to touch the motors to ensure temperatures were normal as well. Everything in engine room upper level seemed to be fine and I made my way down the ladder to the next level.

As I made my way aft, I started hearing an unusual noise. At first it sounded like rubbing, and it was coming from the back of the engine room. I walked back to investigate. It appeared to be coming from shaft alley. This was an area in the back of the engine room where the large rotating propellor shaft exited the pressure hull. As I got closer to the source of the noise, it sounded more like someone running on a treadmill. It didn't make any sense to me. We had treadmills but they were in the missile compartment. I put down my coffee and headed to shaft alley to search for the source of the noise.

As I came down the aft ladder, I saw something I didn't expect. It took me a few seconds to register what I was seeing because it was so surreal. In front of my eyes, I saw a young sailor holding on to two light fixtures and running on the rotating propellor shaft. The noise I heard was his sneakers hitting the shaft. He was startled by my appearance and looked over at me. I recognized the sailor right away because he worked for me, and I wasn't surprised who it was.

"McKinley! What the hell are you doing?!" I yelled. The young sailor jumped down and came over to me. I proceeded to chew him out for doing such a stupid thing. I read him the riot act and explained that his actions were potentially dangerous to him and the ship. When I asked him why he did it, he answered in typical McKinley fashion. He shrugged his shoulders, smiled, and said, "I don't know. I just wondered if I could do it."

Petty Officer McKinley was a third-class petty officer who worked in my division. He was a brilliant electronics technician who could troubleshoot any electrical problem. He was also one of the best reactor operators on the boat. I had stood dozens of watches with him in maneuvering over two patrols. He was a highly capable sailor and an important member of my team, but he was also full of mischief.

McKinley was small in stature, and one of his many skills was

Develop a "No Escape" Mindset

disappearing during field day. Every Saturday morning was field day on the *Tennessee*. That meant all sailors who were not on duty cleaned the boat. From bow to stern, every area of the ship was allocated to a division for cleaning. My division was assigned to clean engine room upper level. As an officer, my task was to ensure everyone was present and cleaning the assigned space. That was my job on paper. After two patrols, I realized my real role was trying to find where McKinley was hiding. He loved to discover new places to go to avoid his cleaning duties.

The first time it happened I went on a wild goose chase. I looked all over the engine room for him only to discover he had jammed himself in the overhead space above some ducting. I had walked by him dozens of times before I decided to look up. When I did, I saw only a sliver of his blue poopy suit uniform crammed in the overhead space. It took him almost ten minutes to get down from his perch. When I asked him what he was doing up there, he just smiled and said, "Cleaning, sir."

On one especially boring midwatch in maneuvering, I had the watch with McKinley as my reactor operator. He decided to entertain himself in a highly unusual way. He started cleaning the dust out of all the cracks and crevices of the reactor control panel. As engineering officer of the watch, I didn't care so long as the conditions of reactor and engine room didn't change. I was busy reviewing my notes for my officer of the deck qualification. About halfway through the watch, McKinley handed me something and said, "Here, sir." I instinctively reached out until I noticed he was handing me a part he had just taken off the panel.

"McKinley! Put that back!" I yelled. "What were you thinking?!"

As he reinstalled the part, McKinley just smiled and said, "I was thinking you would probably react that way."

There was never a dull moment leading a sailor like Petty Officer McKinley. His actions reminded me of something funny I learned in college. I had read that in 1894, the *Army Officer's Guide* had included the following warning for officers when dealing with soldiers: "Enlisted men are…extremely cunning and sly, and bear considerable watching." While this isn't true for most sailors, McKinley fit that description perfectly. That's just how he was wired. He was a brilliant young man who had a whimsical curiosity and loved pushing boundaries. He probably wouldn't have lasted long in corporate America.

Most company bosses don't want to deal with challenging employees like McKinley. They are under pressure to deliver results, and if someone can't perform or has behavior issues, managers have many options to address the problem. In many cases, problem employees are put on performance improvement plans or fired. They are also transferred to other departments. On the *Tennessee*, however, we didn't have that luxury. Whether we liked it or not, we were stuck with the sailors who were assigned to us.

Instead of writing off or ignoring challenging personnel, we had to learn how to accomplish the mission with the people we had. That meant getting to know them and learning what truly motivated them. Even though McKinley was a master at finding ways to get in trouble, I recognized he was both brilliant and bored. He needed to be challenged. His antics almost always occurred during times when he was bored, field day being at the top of his list. To address this, I got him involved with the more complex maintenance and troubleshooting work in the division. I also assigned him to help train new reactor operators. For McKinley, I learned that when his mind was busy, his need to act out went away.

Developing a "no escape" mindset means not writing off or ignoring your most challenging employees. It's about getting the best out of *all* the people on your team. It comes down to getting to know each of your employees and learning what makes them tick. There is no such thing as a one-size-fits-all approach to leading people. Every person is different and must be led in a unique way. We all have a McKinley working for us. It's our job as leaders to find ways to maximize their potential.

THE BUSINESS WORLD: LOBSTERFEST

I'm not sure what got into me. I was excited about the progress we were making in the plant. We had just completed a year without a lost-time accident. This milestone was significant considering our past performance. Still, I thought we could get even better. When I got up to speak to the 250 employees gathered for the all-hands meeting, I didn't really have a plan. I just knew I wanted to say something to challenge them and I wanted to make it fun. What came out of my mouth surprised everyone, including me.

It was May and, as a New Englander, the warmer weather always brought back fond memories of the summer picnics and lobster bakes we used to have growing up. My favorite food has always been lobster, especially lobster rolls. Maybe I was thinking about my childhood when I got up to speak; I'm not really sure. All I know is that after I congratulated the workforce for completing a year without a lost-time accident, I offered up a challenge.

"If you can get to 1,000,000 hours without a lost-time accident, I'll throw a party, and it will be massive. I'll fly live lobsters in from Maine. We will have steaks, corn on the cob, and apple pie for dessert. We'll set up tents on the front lawn and cater the whole thing. If you can accomplish this goal, which has never been done here before, we'll have the biggest party this plant has ever seen!" I could see heads nodding and smiles breaking out. Employees started clapping and cheering. They were up for the challenge. That was exactly the response I wanted to see. I was grinning ear-to-ear as I made my way back to my seat.

I was still smiling when I sat down next to the human resource manager in the front row. When I looked over, however, I noticed she wasn't happy. "What?" I whispered.

"A massive party, huh? How are you going to pull that off?" she asked.

I considered her point and conceded. "I'm not really sure," I said. "But I have a year to figure it out. And I will." There was no way I would back off this promise.

One of the most important things you learn on an operational warship at sea is that words matter. If a sailor told me a valve was shut, I knew it was shut. When I told the captain that the ship was prepared to go to periscope depth, it was ready. Our words had meaning. Everything on the boat had to be carried out with precision and accuracy. One incorrect action could create catastrophic consequences for both the ship and crew. We depended on each other for our very lives. So when we said we would do something, we did it without exception.

That's the thing about having a "no escape" mindset. When you make a commitment, you follow through every time. This is a rare trait in the business world. Sadly, the things people say don't have much value because many people don't follow through on their promises. Many say things casually with no intention of meeting those commitments. This is why the level of trust in many companies is so low. I've learned that the way you build trust as a leader is by being a person whose words matter, by being a person who does what you say. In this case, once those words came out of my mouth, I knew I would deliver on my promise when we reached our goal. There was no escape from my commitment.

It's similar to the concept of burning boats. Sun Tzu, in *The Art of War*, said, "When your army has crossed the border, you should burn your boats and bridges, in order to make it clear to everybody that you have no hankering after home." When you make a commitment to your team, you need to burn the boats behind you. You need to eliminate every means of excuse and escape. When I made the commitment to host the biggest party this plant had ever seen, I knew it was set in stone. Even though we still had the task of getting through another year without a lost-time accident, I began planning the party that afternoon.

As it turned out, I'm glad I did because the employees at this plant delivered another year of perfect safety performance. I had established what business author Jim Collins referred to as a "big hairy audacious goal" and they delivered. We reached 1,000,000 hours without a lost-time accident. We became one of the safest plants in the company, thanks to the hard work and dedication of this workforce. It was now time to celebrate.

I had arranged every detail to match exactly what I had promised the employees. We had large tents set up on the front lawn with tables for all the employees. We hired a caterer who had set up all the equipment to cook everything on site. The most important thing, however, was the 400 live lobsters I had flown in from Maine for the event. As I watched the caterers setting up all the equipment for the party, I had to smile. It was exactly how I imagined it would look when I made that promise more than a year ago. The vision had now become reality.

The party was perfect, and I enjoyed every minute of it. I especially loved watching employees learn how to eat lobster. For many, it was their first time. The day was filled with fun, laughter, and great food. It's my favorite memory of that plant and the people I worked with there. Together, we reached a world-class level of performance that few plants ever achieve, and we all celebrated it in a big way. We also celebrated it in the best way – with each other.

Developing a "no escape" mindset is powerful. It's all about not taking the easy way out. Whether it's a bad coworker, a challenging employee, or even a personal commitment, the best way to get things done is to not back down or walk away from the challenge. It's about getting along with people that you have differences with and working to find common ground. It's also about developing thick skin and not being offended so easily. If you can learn to laugh at your mistakes and take yourself a little less seriously, you will become more resilient. In an increasingly divided world, a "no escape" mindset can be a superpower.

THE BOTTOM LINE

Key Points

- Learn to work with people you have differences with.
- Learn to compromise, find common ground, and seek win-win outcomes.
- Develop a higher tolerance for people with different opinions and personalities.
- Adopt a forgive-and-forget mindset.
- Don't take yourself so seriously.
- Have thick skin, be tough, and be resilient.
- Get the best out of *all* the people on your team, even the challenging ones.
- Follow through on your commitments every time.

Tweetable Quotes

Tweet the following quotes with these hashtags: #allinthesameboat #noescape

"When there is no escape from a bad coworker, you find ways to work together."

"If more people had the opportunity to serve on a deployed submarine for three months, they would have a lot more tolerance for people with different opinions and beliefs."

"In the tight spaces of a submarine at sea, you can't let problems linger and go unaddressed."

"If something bothers you, the last thing you want is to let a submariner know it."

"If you can't laugh at yourself, you'd make a terrible submariner."

"Working to resolve conflicts, looking for common ground, and having a forgive-and-forget mindset will help you be a better leader."

"Developing a 'no escape' mindset means not writing off or ignoring your most challenging employees."

"The way you build trust as a leader is by being a person who does what you say."

Develop a "No Escape" Mindset

Questions to Ponder

1. Who are you having trouble working with and why? How can the "no escape" mindset change that?

2. Name something that happened to you at work and still bothers you today. How can you forgive and forget?

3. Who is your most challenging employee? How can you get the most out of that person?

4. What commitments have you made to your team? What are you doing to ensure you don't back down from those commitments?

Chapter 7.

Run Your Ship Like a Captain

*The three most powerful men in the world
— the president of the United States of America,
the president of the Russian Republic,
and the captain of a United States ballistic missile submarine.*

— Opening monologue, *Crimson Tide*

Questioning Authority

"Alert One! Alert One!" The 1MC rang out through the boat. I was in the officer's study trying to wrap my head around the *Tennessee's* complex hydraulic systems. The message was a welcomed distraction. I was excited to respond to my first emergency action message. I was one of the six officers assigned to decode these messages when they were received in the radio room. I was also the newest member of the team.

I was on my second patrol and had attended emergency action message training during our last off-crew. I was looking forward to using my newfound skills and providing a valuable function on the boat. Emergency action messages are critically important. They are used to communicate between the National Command Authority and submarine captains regarding the use of missiles. If you've seen the 1995 movie *Crimson Tide*, you probably know what these are.

That entire movie is based on a disagreement about an emergency action message. The seasoned captain, played by Gene Hackman, and his new executive officer, played by Denzel Washington, fight over what to do with a garbled radio message. The struggle over whether or not to deploy the boat's missiles divides the crew, and a mutiny eventually occurs. As you can probably imagine, this is all just Hollywood fantasy because the rules for handling these messages are unambiguous.

I rushed to the radio room, knowing the first two officers there would get to decode the message, and I was eager to show off my new skills. I was the first to arrive, soon followed by another one of the junior officers. The entire decoding procedure is a carefully choreographed event, and we carried it out without a single issue. We then moved to control to authenticate the message with the captain and executive officer.

Before I continue, let me explain something about our skipper. Our commanding officer was a seasoned undersea warrior. He was a captain on his second command – salty and larger than life. He had been making deployments for nearly 20 years and was one of the fleet's best commanding officers. I was honored to serve under him. He demanded excellence from his crews and we delivered. As a young junior officer just starting my second patrol, I both respected and feared him. And I wasn't the only one.

My partner and I presented the decoded message to the captain and executive officer. After we went through a precise script, we both repeated the words, "The message is authentic." The executive officer reviewed the message and our decoding work and repeated, "The message is authentic." The captain looked through everything and said, "I concur."

At that point, I'm not sure what came over me. Maybe because I had just been through the training, or perhaps I was just eager to show off my new skills. But for some reason, I proceeded to tell the captain he was wrong. In front of everyone in the control room, I said, "Actually, Captain, you're supposed to say, 'the message is authentic' as well."

He didn't say a word but the look he gave me sent chills down my spine. I imagine it's the same feeling you probably get after poking a 600-pound grizzly bear with a stick. I knew I was in trouble. He didn't break eye contact and thundered for everyone to hear, "The message is authentic. This is a drill. Secure from the drill." As he turned to leave control, he looked back at me and, in a booming voice, said, "Mr. Rennie, in my stateroom now."

Everybody in control looked at me for several moments, then looked away. There wasn't a person on that boat who wanted to be in my shoes right then. As a 24-year-old unqualified junior officer, I had just questioned the captain of a nuclear ballistic missile submarine at sea during the Cold War. I had just poked the bear.

Like a man walking to the gallows, I left control and walked slowly down to the captain's stateroom, wondering the whole time what was going to happen. I replayed the scene in my head a dozen times. For the life of me, I couldn't understand why I would question a man I respected so much in front of the entire watch team. I was both confused and embarrassed. I had never even been in the captain's stateroom. In my mind, he was a giant and his stateroom was his lair. I had no idea what would happen to me, but I knew it wouldn't be good for my naval career. I had committed a cardinal sin by questioning the captain – and I would now have to face the consequences.

I knocked on his door and waited. After a few moments, he yelled, "Enter!" I stepped in and stood at attention. "Shut the door!" he bellowed. I did and returned to attention. "Mr. Rennie," he said, "I've been watching you. You're pretty smart but you don't know everything." He continued, "This is my ship, and you'll become a great officer if you spend more time listening to me and less time telling me what to do. Do I make myself clear?"

I answered smartly, "Yes, sir!"

He locked eyes on me and then said, "Dismissed!"

The words that echoed through my head after I left his stateroom were, "I've been watching you," "you're pretty smart," and "you'll become a great officer." I suddenly realized I was beaming with pride. I had expected some type of punishment. Instead, the captain – a man I both feared and respected – just told me that I would become a great officer one day. Up to this point I didn't think he even knew who I was. I had spent the past six months desperately trying to become useful and not be a burden on the crew. I was still raw and unqualified, but the captain saw something in me. He saw my potential. He also gave me the "cheat code" to become a great officer – spend more time listening to him.

On a submarine at sea the captain is ultimately responsible for the ship, the mission, and the crew. It is a tremendous responsibility. During the Cold War the fate of the world was riding on his shoulders, but he couldn't do the job alone. He needed a competent crew and skilled officers to lead them and, just like a college sports team, the players would change every year and every patrol. There would be some experienced, returning players, but there would also be a batch of new, raw recruits. Like a coach, the captain had to evaluate talent and build the team. He pushed us hard because his career, his life, his country, and the lives of his crew depended on it.

I took the captain's words to heart. From that point on I listened to everything he said, and I learned from his deep experience in submarine operations. In time, he picked me for some of the most challenging assignments. He selected me to be the geoplot operator during battle stations, essentially becoming his eyes and ears during torpedo operations. I was named the officer of the deck for the maneuvering watch and the midwatch. He put me in charge when the stakes were the highest. And in the high-pressure world of a submarine on patrol, he took the time to teach me. Like a father teaching a son, he explained why things needed to be done in a certain way. He was still as tough as nails but the more time I served under him, the more I began to understand his intentions.

The most valuable lesson I learned during this time was that the leader is ultimately responsible for the mission and the team. For the team to be successful, the leader must make sure each person is trained and skilled in their position, especially new employees. The leader is also responsible for observing and evaluating talent. He creates the next generation of leaders by identifying employees with leadership potential and giving them challenging jobs and stretch assignments to assess their performance. Ultimately the leader becomes a mentor to the best employees, providing direct instruction on how to become even better so that they can take his place one day.

Ready or Not

It was still pitch dark when I climbed to the bridge and continued preparations to get underway. "Maneuvering, bridge. What's the status of the reactor?" I asked.

I was desperate to get everything ready before the VIPs arrived. It was only 0500 so I still had plenty of time. It was a chilly morning and I could see my breath as I exhaled, but the weather reports called for a nearly perfect day with calm winds and warm weather. The captain had selected me to prepare the boat for the long-anticipated "dependents cruise." Today 75 friends and family of our crew would board the *Tennessee*, and I had the watch. I was not only responsible for getting the boat ready but I was also responsible for taking her to sea. I would be the maneuvering watch officer of the deck as we departed Kings Bay for the open ocean.

I had been the officer of the deck on the maneuvering watch several times. I wouldn't say I was an expert but I knew what to expect. This morning, however, I was in entirely uncharted waters. I had never prepped the boat for sea like I was doing today and certainly had no experience preparing for 75 civilians who would be our guests. I had never even been on a dependents cruise before. I felt a bit overwhelmed and wondered quietly why the skipper had even given me this assignment. There were far more experienced officers in the wardroom. Yet, he had delegated the full authority of this job to me. He wasn't even on board yet. As far as I knew, he was still at home while I struggled to get everything ready.

I continued through my checklists without incident, and by 0545 the guests began arriving on the pier. My wife, parents, and in-laws would be part of that crowd but I was too busy to look for them. I had a job to do, and I knew that at 0700 we would be casting off all lines and heading to sea. The prep work was hard enough, but coordinating the tugboats and maneuvering through the tight channel would take all my concentration and effort. This day would be fun for many, but for me it was all business.

Once the captain arrived, he welcomed the visitors and everyone got on board for the day's events. Around 0645, the captain finally made his way to the bridge. I think he saw the relief in my eyes when I saw him. All morning the weight of the world had been on my shoulders, and I was genuinely glad to see him. It was not unlike the captain to give his junior officers challenging assignments to see how they performed. I was just happy he would be there as we departed the channel.

Instead of asking for a formal report, he just said, "How'd it go this morning, Mr. Rennie?" I gave him a brief update on the preparations while he took in the full scene of this powerful warship preparing to get underway. He had the look of a man who was truly in his element and knew his time in command was limited. I felt like he was considering that his days of daring and adventure would eventually end, and he was soaking it all in. I could tell he genuinely loved his job and this short experience with him on the bridge made me appreciate the moment as well. We were both doing something that few people would ever get to do: We were taking a nuclear submarine to sea.

He looked directly at me and asked, "But how do you feel?"

I answered honestly, "Well, Captain, better now that you're here."

He just smiled and nodded.

As I worked through my checklists and continued preparations, I was about to receive a surprise I hadn't considered. Beyond the usual sounds of tugs, heavy equipment, and the crew busily preparing the *Tennessee* for sea, I thought I heard a familiar voice. Someone was coming up the ladder and trying to get to the bridge. In the morning shadows I couldn't quite make out who it was. Then the voice said clearly, "Where do I put my feet? What do I hold on to?" To my surprise, it was my mother making her way to the bridge.

The captain had invited my parents and my wife to be on the bridge as special guests as we departed Kings Bay. My parents would be riding on the port fairwater planes and my wife would be on the flying bridge with the captain. It was a position of honor for them but it created a rush of nervousness for me. *What was the captain thinking?* I thought. He knew I would need my full concentration to transit the narrow channel successfully, but now I would be doing it under the watchful eyes of my parents and my wife. Like a golfer preparing to hit a ball with the added pressure of an entire crowd looking on, I wondered, *Is he purposely ratcheting up the level of difficulty for me? Is he testing me to see how I'll perform under this added pressure?* I smiled because I already knew the answers to these questions.

Luckily for me, the morning commute through the tight channel and out to sea was uneventful. I had been the officer of the deck for the maneuvering watch enough times that I was beginning to get comfortable in the role. My orders were crisp and I knew what to expect. I anticipated each bend in the channel as well as the slow, lumbering performance of the *Tennessee*. I lined up the channel markers with precision and we powered through the turns in the early morning sunlight. It was a perfect morning, just as the forecasts had predicted. The warm morning sun lit all of our faces in a golden glow. I looked back at my wife standing next to the captain. She was smiling and taking it all in. My parents and all the other VIPs on the fairwater planes seemed to be enjoying themselves as well. For each of them this was a once-in-a-lifetime experience, a moment they would always treasure. As it turned out, it was for me as well.

This morning was the first time I felt entirely sure of my decisions as officer of the deck. I knew what to expect, and it felt like I could see things before they happened. In football, they say that new quarterbacks get to a point where the game "slows down" for them. The same thing happened to me that day. The entire watch slowed down for me, and the 560-foot warship went precisely where I wanted it to go. The captain seemed to sense this change in me also. Usually he'd be coaching his junior officers through this difficult evolution but instead he was letting me lead. I thought about what he had asked me earlier, "How do you feel?" I smiled because I understood his question now. I felt confident.

The captain knew what he was doing when he gave me the watch that morning. He had delegated the full authority to me to get the *Tennessee* ready for sea, but he always maintained the responsibility for making sure it happened. He gave me a stretch assignment, something I'd never done before, to test me. He wanted to evaluate my training. He wanted to see how I would handle myself in a pressure-filled situation. It was similar to the hundreds of drills we ran on patrol. The captain was always pressure-testing us and evaluating us to make sure we knew what to do in every situation. In the process the game slowed down for us. We developed muscle memory and we gained confidence.

An important lesson I learned from the Navy was to delegate authority but maintain responsibility. On the *Tennessee*, the captain was entirely responsible for everything. Ultimately it was the captain's fault for not training the crew and supervising them properly if anything bad happened. This is how the Navy viewed responsibility. But they also understood the importance of delegating authority. For people to feel empowered and challenged, they must be given the full authority to get the job done. Assigning me the duty to prepare the boat for sea for the dependents cruise was far outside my comfort zone. It was beyond my capabilities at the time, but the captain delegated the authority to me and stepped away. He understood that growth always happens outside your comfort zone.

If you contrast this to corporate America, you'll find that most bosses do just the opposite: They delegate responsibility but maintain authority. They hold their employees responsible if anything goes wrong, but they rarely give them the full authority they need to get the job done. As a result, the boss centralizes all the power and very little learning occurs in the team. This setup ultimately leads to frustrated employees. They find themselves stuck in the futile position of being held responsible for results they don't have the authority to achieve.

These bosses miss out on another important aspect of delegating authority as well – the chance to evaluate the employee. There was no doubt in my mind that the captain was testing me that day. He assigned me a job I was not fully ready for, and he increased the difficulty by inviting my family to the bridge for the maneuvering watch. He wanted to see how I performed. Think about the question he asked: "How do you feel?" This was not a question of someone concerned about the state of the ship. He was concerned about the state of his employee. He wanted to know if I was overwhelmed or if I was feeling confident. The best leaders test and evaluate their teams to observe their performance and build confidence in their employees.

Under Attack

"Shots fired topside!"

The topside watch's nervous voice rang out over the 1MC throughout the boat. I heard both his voice and what sounded like automatic rifle fire.

What in the world? I thought. There wasn't supposed to be anything happening tonight. I knew this couldn't be a drill, and things were about to get real.

Most nights standing watch as the ship's duty officer in port are boring and uneventful, but this was not like most nights. I was set up in the officer's study. This is where I usually spent my nights when I had the in-port duty. It was a central place where sailors and shipyard workers could easily find me. And if I got tired, I could nap on the orange Naugahyde-covered benches in the study. The junior officers affectionately called this a "Nauga-nap." It wasn't uncommon for the ship's duty officer to doze off once or twice during the long night watches.

We had a few maintenance items going on that night, and I had just signed off on a large electrical system tagout. But for the most part, I expected this to be a quiet watch. Before I took the watch, I reviewed both the ship's plan of the day and the base's plan of the day. I knew there was nothing unusual going on. I had about eight hours to kill before I was relieved, and I was content to relax and catch up on some reading. I wasn't prepared for what I just heard.

"Shots fired topside!"

When I heard those words repeated, my adrenaline spiked. I was already on my way to control, where I grabbed the 1MC microphone. As I had been trained to do, I gave the order to protect the boat: "Repel boarders! Repel boarders! This is not a drill!" I knew this would put a plan in motion that would seal all the hatches and prevent anyone from getting inside the boat, but I still had no idea what was going on.

The small skeleton crew on the ship that night moved quickly to seal all the hatches, open up the small-arms locker, and distribute weapons. We had trained on this so often that the crew's actions were almost automatic, but I was still uneasy. I kept thinking this wasn't a drill and something terrible was happening. The topside's nervous voice kept replaying in my head. I needed to find out what was going on.

I rang the topside watch and asked, "Topside, ship's duty officer. What is going on up there?"

The young sailor responded, "I don't know, sir. I see soldiers moving towards the dry dock firing weapons."

I knew this wasn't good. There wasn't supposed to be any training on base this evening. I quickly put the phone back in the cradle and moved to the #1 scope to see for myself. As I rotated the heavy periscope 90 degrees towards the base, I was shocked by what I saw. Dozens of troops in camouflage were moving and firing on the dry dock west of the main pier. Something was seriously going on. My immediate concern was for the *Tennessee* and her crew. We had trained for this type of scenario but I had never expected it to happen, especially in our home port.

I zoomed in with the scope to see who these soldiers were and noticed it right away. Luckily for me, I spent a week training with Marines at Camp Pendleton in California as a midshipman. I had been issued an M16 and participated in several mock battles where we fired blanks at "enemy" soldiers. As I looked carefully at the men running towards the dry dock, I noticed the red blank-firing adapters on the barrel of each gun. These were U.S. Marines and this was some sort of training. I knew right away that the ship wasn't in any danger, but now I had other questions. Someone had royally screwed up by not making us aware of this planned exercise. These Marines were firing blanks, but the *Tennessee's* sailors were now carrying weapons and live ammo.

It didn't take me long to realize the condition we were now in: The Marines were conducting a drill, but we were not. I had to deescalate this situation quickly before anyone got hurt. I made the snap decision to secure from "repel boarders" even though I didn't know exactly what was going on. I announced on the 1MC that this was just an exercise and to secure from the drill. The crew reopened the hatches and worked quickly to return the *Tennessee* to its normal "in port" configuration. I remained in the control room until I received reports that all of the small arms and ammo had been accounted for and returned to the small-arms locker. As I sat there, the adrenaline in my body slowly dissipated, but what returned was anger. Someone failed to inform the boats on the main pier about this exercise, which could have turned deadly.

I focused all of my rage on the one person who should have prevented this from happening – the base duty officer. In my mind he was responsible for informing all the other duty officers of this exercise. It was his fault for not warning us and putting us in this potentially dangerous situation. My anger grew as I stormed back down to the officer's study, where we had the STU-III. The STU-III was a secure telephone which provided encrypted verbal communications when we were in port. I dialed the base duty officer and waited.

"Base duty officer, Lieutenant Commander Gallo speaking."

The calm voice on the other end of the line only made me angrier. I introduced myself, then asked if there was a security exercise at the dry dock this evening, even though I already knew the answer. The base duty officer confirmed that the Marine detachment was currently conducting a full-scale training exercise. His matter-of-fact tone only added fuel to my fire. In a far-too-sarcastic way, I asked if he had any plans to inform the boats on the waterfront about this exercise. The base duty officer caught my attitude and decided to pull rank.

"It was at the dry dock, so it shouldn't affect you, Lieutenant." He pronounced *Lieutenant* very slowly to make sure I understood he outranked me.

Now I'm not sure exactly what happened next, but I remember hearing a voice that sounded a lot like mine suggesting that the lieutenant commander should get off his "sorry, incompetent, lazy ass" and do his job before someone got hurt. I also remember hearing the ugly sound of broken plastic as the STU-III handset was slammed so hard onto the receiver that it shattered into several pieces.

When I came back to my senses, I looked down at the damaged phone and tried to recall what I had just said. *This isn't good*, I thought. It was well past midnight and now I had to call the captain at home. I needed to tell him I had initiated a repel boarders, chewed out a senior officer, and destroyed a $2,000 secure telephone. I knew this wasn't going to be fun. My night was going from bad to worse.

When I woke the captain, I was surprised to find him in good spirits. I told him what had transpired and how I had launched a repel boarders action based on what was happening around the ship. He immediately agreed with my decision and asked me if I had confronted the base duty officer. He knew who was ultimately responsible for this.

"Well, sir, that's the problem," I said sheepishly. "I might have called the base duty officer an incompetent, lazy ass, and he's a lieutenant commander. You're probably going to hear about it."

The captain laughed out loud. "I would have done the same thing. Don't worry about it." His reaction was better than expected, so I figured I'd hit him with the rest of the bad news.

"And another thing, Captain," I said. "After confronting the base duty officer, I slammed the phone down so hard, the handset shattered. It'll have to be replaced. That's my fault, sir."

The captain took it all in and then said, "Don't worry about it. Overall, you did the right thing tonight. I've got your back."

And I knew he did.

This was the last time we ever spoke about the incident. The captain kept his word and had my back. He took care of the situation with the base duty officer and the busted phone. He understood my anger for what had happened that night. Even though I should have been disciplined for disrespecting a senior officer and breaking the phone, he protected me because he knew my intentions were right.

The captain had just demonstrated another important aspect of delegating authority: the idea of supporting your employees when they make honest mistakes. That night things didn't go as planned, and I had to deal with a situation that I didn't anticipate. While most of my actions were correct, I should have kept my cool with the base duty officer. I knew I had screwed up and deserved to be disciplined for my actions. The captain saw the bigger picture, though. Like him, I cared deeply for the safety of the boat and the crew. I had unleashed my anger on the one person who put that safety in jeopardy. While my actions still weren't justified, he understood the intentions behind them and backed me up.

It's hard to describe in words the feeling you get when you know you have a boss who has your back. While I already had a deep respect for my captain, my loyalty to him went through the roof. I knew I had an excellent commanding officer, and I would do anything to make him proud. Instead of throwing me under the bus for my actions in order to protect his career and reputation, he defended me. He stood up for me because he put his people and the mission above himself.

Unfortunately, this type of leadership behavior is uncommon. Many bosses don't appreciate the power of supporting their employees. Too many won't stand up for their team members when mistakes are made. In situations like this many managers abandon their people to protect their reputations. Sadly, these bosses place a higher priority on their careers than on their people or mission. When problems occur, they walk away and let the employee take the fall.

The lesson I learned from my captain that day is that when great leaders delegate authority, they always maintain responsibility. They understand the leader is ultimately responsible for the people and the mission. When things go wrong, they don't abdicate that responsibility to protect their career – they own it. They back up their employees when honest mistakes happen. They step up and protect their employees and, in turn, create loyal followers.

THE BUSINESS WORLD: NO TIME LIKE THE PRESENT

"You have six months to do it."

Those were the last words our division president said to me as we wrapped up the meeting.

Six months? I thought as I walked back to my car. *That's impossible.* There was no way we could move a manufacturing operation from Kentucky to North Carolina in six months. The building addition at the existing North Carolina plant would take more than a year to complete. It was an unreasonable request, but the division president explained how it would save the company millions if we could quickly combine the operations.

As I drove the familiar 72 miles back to the North Carolina plant, I thought about how I would break the news to the leadership team. I knew they were going to see it the same way I saw it – as an impossible mission. I had a talented team. They had done some fantastic things in the past, but this request was well beyond our capabilities (or the capabilities of any group, for that matter.) When I was 15 minutes out, I called my assistant and asked her to assemble the staff for a meeting as soon as I arrived.

"Alright, here's the deal," I said. "Instead of two years, the schedule for moving the Kentucky plant has just been compressed. We now have six months to get it done."

I figured the best way to break the news was to rip the Band-Aid off – and the response was just what I expected. I lost count of how many times I heard the word "impossible" as they reacted to the news. They were going through the same emotions I went through on my drive. They were surprised, shocked, angry, frustrated, and skeptical. How could they be asked to do something like this? It was a ridiculous task.

I let them vent, knowing it was just part of the process. James Prochaska and Carlo DiClemente created the *Stages of Change Model* in the late 1970s to explain how people deal with change. They called the first stage precontemplation, characterized by denial and a desire to maintain the status quo. That is where we were and my only hope was to get to the next stage by the end of this first meeting. I hoped we could at least begin thinking about how we could accomplish this challenging assignment.

I remembered something I had heard about Walt Disney's leadership style. He was a leader who hated negativity. He believed in the philosophy of "yes, if" instead of "no, because." I was hearing a lot of negativity, so I decided to try a little Disney magic to see if it would work with my team. I said, "Instead of saying this is impossible, let's consider that it is possible. Finish this sentence for me: To be able to move the plant in six months, we need what?"

That opened the door to a lot of discussion and debate. Then one of the managers, who had been quiet the whole time, finally spoke up.

"We don't have space and the building addition won't be ready for a year. So it's simple. We need a temporary building."

That little spark shifted the entire conversation. Instead of hearing the word "impossible," I started hearing positive discussions on how we could make the move if we could build a temporary building or lease a facility. The team was suddenly energized by shifting the way we were thinking about the problem. By the end of the meeting we had moved to the second stage of change, the contemplation stage. We were all considering the possibilities if we had additional manufacturing space in or around our existing North Carolina plant. I ended the meeting by telling the team to keep thinking about the problem. We would reconvene the following morning.

I went back to my office and thought about the challenge we had before us. When I first became a manufacturing plant manager 10 years earlier, I used to think I needed to have all the answers. What I learned over that decade is that it is always better to bring problems like this to employees and be willing to listen to the quietest voice in the room. The collective wisdom of a team is always more significant than the ideas of one manager. Today's discussion was further proof of that. A few words from a quiet meeting participant had opened a door of possibilities I hadn't even considered. As I thought about these things, I was interrupted by a knock on my door.

"Can I come in?" It was my manufacturing engineering manager,

Tom. He was excited. "I just spoke with a company that has 50,000 square feet of manufacturing space that we can lease for a year. It's two towns over but I think it will work. We have an appointment to see the building tomorrow at eight." I smiled. What seemed like an impossible task earlier in the day was starting to look doable.

The next day we toured the space. In what seemed like a miracle, the building was exactly what we needed. It had the right layout, power, loading docks, a break room, and everything else we needed. It was also available and surprisingly affordable. As we walked through the facility, we all began to feel like the six-month target was entirely possible. Still, it would take a detailed plan, flawlessly executed, to make it happen. It would also require the right leader to run the project.

I had worked with Tom for several years in three different locations. He had proven himself a capable leader and project manager, but this endeavor was unlike any he had ever done for me before. This project would be a highly visible stretch assignment for him with little room for error. Moving a manufacturing operation on a tight schedule would take his absolute best. I could have looked for more experienced project managers in the company; however, I trusted him and wanted to give him this opportunity.

I decided to delegate 100% of the authority for the project to him. I felt confident he would build a solid plan and do his best to execute it with precision. I looked forward to seeing his capabilities. I also made sure he understood that I would maintain full responsibility for the outcome of the project. As the leader of the organization, I would never push this responsibility to anyone else. If the project failed, it was ultimately my fault. I made sure he understood that whatever happened, I had his back.

General George Patton once famously said, "Never tell people how to do things. Tell them what to do, and they will surprise you with their ingenuity." That's the best way to describe what happened on this project. Not only was the project executed on budget and within the compressed time frame required by the division president, but Tom also led the project with tremendous creativity and ingenuity. He made several critical decisions to make sure he completed the project on time. The most impressive idea was one that did the most to compress the schedule.

Tom decided to set up the temporary plant exactly how it existed in Kentucky. In other words, the equipment layout would be identical – to the inch – as it had been operating for years in Kentucky. He had the project team tape out the entire production line on the temporary facility floor so they knew exactly where to place all the power lines and air hoses. Before they moved anything, the team thoroughly prepared the temporary building to receive each piece of equipment. The machines were then simply unplugged from Kentucky and plugged back in when they arrived at the new location. This simple idea allowed the project to move with incredible speed.

In the end, the project was a huge success. What was considered an impossible request was carried out with perfection. Although he never mentioned it, I don't believe the division president ever honestly thought what he was asking for could be done. But there's an important lesson here as well: As leaders, we sometimes need to challenge our teams to do the impossible. Often it's the only way real breakthroughs in thinking and action will ever occur. When we challenge our teams, they will always surprise us with their ingenuity and creativity.

Pressure Test

I was nervous but trying not to show it. Once the previous EOOW left maneuvering, it suddenly hit me. I was in charge of an operating nuclear power plant at sea. The entire crew was depending on me to do my job with precision. I was standing my first watch as EOOW, and the weight of that responsibility suddenly felt crushing.

I had completed my qualifications as EOOW and EDO (engineering duty officer) after months of study, observation, and supervision. I was now ready to fly solo. I passed the engineering board examination, but it was tough. The captain and ship's engineer asked me several difficult, off-the-wall technical questions that I struggled to answer. At one point I thought it was over, but somehow I made it through. After two years of training, I was finally qualified as a nuclear submarine engineering officer. The responsibility of the *USS Tennessee's* engine room and everyone in it was mine for the next six hours.

The work I had put in over the last two years was almost unimaginable. It was undoubtedly the hardest thing I'd ever done. In every nuclear power training stage, officers failed out of the program – but I was still here. I had survived nuke school, prototype training, submarine school, and the past six months on the *Tennessee*. I had put in all that work to qualify as the newest EOOW on the boat. It was strange to think I was finally here. It felt almost surreal that I was no longer training but now doing the job.

As the watch went on, I began to feel more comfortable. The nervousness I felt when I first took over the watch had subsided and I slipped into the routine of operating one of the most advanced engine rooms in the world. I had stood so many under-instruction watches that I was familiar with all the regular activities that needed to be done. I was also confident knowing I had qualified watchstanders all around me. The sailors in the engine room with me were experienced and they weren't going to let me fail. As I quietly performed the job I had trained so hard for, I thought, *This isn't so bad. I've got this.*

About four hours into the watch, everything changed. It started with a 1MC announcement. "This is the captain," he said. "I just want to let everyone know that Ensign Rennie has qualified as the newest engineering officer of the watch. He has worked very hard and has earned the right to stand watch at this important duty station. Please join me in congratulating him. And, Mr. Rennie, keep my plant safe!!"

As soon as he finished the announcement, all hell broke loose. It was a reactor scram. A scram is the sudden shutdown of the nuclear reactor by a rapid insertion of the control rods. For some reason, all the control rods on the *Tennessee's* reactor just dropped and every alarm in maneuvering went off simultaneously. It was absolute chaos. Fortunately, I knew what to do. Recovering the plant after a scram is something I had practiced dozens of times.

I silenced the alarms in maneuvering and picked up the 2MC microphone to start giving orders to the engine room personnel. I was about to give my first command when someone came to the door of maneuvering and snapped a picture of me. *This was all a setup*, I thought as I continued through my immediate actions. The captain wanted to see how I would handle a casualty on my first watch, so he had given the command to scram the reactor. He also wanted to see my reaction to his unannounced drill, so he sent the ship's photographer with a Polaroid to capture the moment.

I recovered the plant in short order and the rest of my watch was uneventful, but I kept thinking about that reactor scram drill. It was a typical move by our captain. His standards were high and he didn't allow anyone to serve in a critical role unless they had proven themselves. He was tough on sailors and even tougher on his officers. The scram was both a test and message. He wanted to see how I handled myself, but he also wanted to remind me never to get too comfortable. As a watch officer, I needed to be ready for anything.

There was another side to the captain as well. His praise over the 1MC was genuine. He was truly proud of me for getting through one of the most challenging technical programs on earth. In a way, he was welcoming me to an elite club. His message over the 1MC was to let me know that I belonged in this club and that he trusted me with "his" plant.

And the photograph? Well, that was just a submarine thing. The captain wanted to record my reaction to the surprise drill right when all the rods hit the reactor's bottom. He would pass around the picture to the other officers and have a good laugh. Everyone in the wardroom, including the captain, had been in that same position. All had been beginners at one point in their career. Sharing the picture with the other officers was my final initiation into the club. The response to the photograph was always the same; they laughed and then proceeded to tell me stories of their first watch. The picture reminded each officer of where he had come from, and it was an affirmation that I belonged as well.

When you run your organization like a captain, you keep your standards high. The employees who fill your most critical roles must be pressure-tested. You need to know how they will perform under pressure. While you can't perform a reactor scram drill, you can find other ways to test your employees to ensure they are up to the task. A simple way is to challenge them either with a stretch assignment or a difficult task. Like my captain, you can observe your employees' responses as they operate out of their comfort zone. This feedback will help you better evaluate employees to make sure you have the right people in your most important roles.

The other thing a captain does is let the rest of the organization know he approves and supports the people in these critical roles. When employees have proven themselves, you need to let the rest of the team know you trust them to do the job and fully support them. In a way, these employees have entered into a circle of trust with you. You trust them to carry out the organization's mission on your behalf. The rest of the team needs to know you have their back.

THE BUSINESS WORLD: CHALLENGING THE STATUS QUO

"When can you get to Florida? I want to meet you and see your plans to grow the business."

Grow the business? That's odd, I thought as I hung up the phone. The company had just hired a senior vice president who was my new boss. He came from one of our competitors. Management at our company thought we needed some outside blood in our division to spark change. I couldn't have agreed more. I was excited to meet him but I kept thinking about his request. Most new managers want to understand the people and business first before diving deep into the growth plans. This guy wanted to talk about them on day one.

The problem was that I didn't have a growth plan. I had a budget and a forecast, but those were just for short-term planning. What my new boss was asking for was a long-term plan. The other thing that bothered me was that I already had about 60% market share on my main product line. Sure, we could grow, but by how much? The last time I checked, monopolies were illegal. Still, I took the time to develop what I felt was a comprehensive plan before booking my trip to the division headquarters in central Florida.

When I arrived for our meeting, I noticed he wanted to get right to business. We spent a little time getting to know each other, but he seemed more interested in seeing my plans. I started by talking about our business and how far we had come. We had gone from about 35% to 60% market share in the past eight years, most of that gain coming in the more recent years. I was confident we could grow even more and listed several ratings and specifications to add to the portfolio that would push us to around 70% eventually.

It was a detailed and realistic plan which I thought would impress him. But as I showed the projected growth curve, I could tell he wasn't happy.

He looked at me and said, "This is great, but what can you do to double your business?"

Double? I thought. *This guy's crazy.* I thought maybe he missed the part of the presentation where I mentioned we already had 60% market share. So I went back and presented the slide that showed our market share growth and explained why we couldn't double our business.

He wasn't buying it. He told me, "You're not thinking correctly. Come back with a plan to double your business."

Frustrated and somewhat embarrassed, I made my way back to the airport to catch a flight home. I kept thinking the rest of the day: *Why does he think I can double my business when I already have 60% market share?* I thought he was nuts. He didn't know anything about our operation, yet he was pushing me for more than what was possible. The more I thought about it, the angrier I got. This trip was a complete waste of time and I could tell the next few years weren't going to be easy.

When I returned to the factory the next day, I gathered the management team for an afternoon brainstorming session. Maybe I was overlooking something. I shared the presentation I had given our new boss and talked about his reaction. I asked my team, "What are we missing? How can we double our business?" Like me, they were confused as well. It didn't seem like the market for our products was large enough to double sales. We debated several ideas for about 30 minutes when our marketing manager finally spoke up.

"Maybe we're thinking about our business wrong." He explained that up to this point we had only talked about how to grow sales of our main product line, which was current and voltage transformers.

"What if we are not in the transformer business but in the business of measuring current and voltage? How big would the market be for products in this category?" he asked.

His observation shifted the direction of the conversation. As it turned out, the market for current and voltage measuring devices was 10 times bigger than that of transformers alone. We could double the size of our business by getting into another type of product that could measure current and voltage. After further discussion, the direction that made the most sense was developing a sensor portfolio. Current and voltage sensing was an emerging technology that could result in a doubling of sales. It turned out my new boss was right all along – I hadn't been thinking correctly.

Several weeks later I presented a new growth plan to my boss. I explained how we could double the size of our business by launching a new line of current and voltage sensors. The technology was straightforward. Plus, we could manufacture the units in our factory by adding just a few pieces of new equipment. He not only approved the plan but also applauded us for thinking differently about the business.

In the end, it took us several years to develop and successfully launch a new family of sensors to the market, but this new technology allowed us to double our business. That one question from my new boss changed everything. He challenged my plans and pushed me to do more than I thought was possible. His refusal to accept the status quo led to a new way of thinking about our business.

Over the years I have thought a lot about that boss and how he pushed us. Did he know there was a way to double our sales or was he just trying to get us to think differently? Did he know the answer or did he just have a good question? I'm more and more convinced that he had no idea if there was a solution to the challenge he put before us but he wanted to see what we would do. He was testing our ability to question our assumptions and think outside the box. He was observing us and seeing if we could take our business to a new level.

Part of running your ship like a captain is challenging your employees to do more than they think is possible. It's about pushing back on their assumptions and making them think differently. The tough questions will give you the chance to observe your employees and see how they respond. To be a great leader, you don't have to have all the answers but you do need to have the right questions.

The Bottom Line

Key Points

- A leader is ultimately responsible for the mission AND the team.
- A leader must ensure each person is skilled and trained in his or her position.
- A leader is responsible for observing, evaluating, and developing employees.
- A leader should delegate authority but always maintain responsibility.
- Stretch assignments provide employees with valuable experience and can boost confidence.
- Leaders who back their employees when honest mistakes happen create loyal followers.
- Employees who fill your most critical roles must be pressure-tested.
- We need to create moments for employees to "surprise" us with their ingenuity.

Tweetable Quotes

Tweet the following quotes with these hashtags: #allinthesameboat #leadlikeacaptain

"The captain is ultimately responsible for the ship, the mission, and the crew."

"The captain continuously pressure-tests the crew, evaluating them to make sure they know what to do in every situation."

"Like a coach, a leader must evaluate talent and build up the team."

"Great leaders use stretch assignments to evaluate how high-potential employees will perform."

"Great leaders are concerned with the state of their employees, not just the state of the business."

"A great leader puts his people and the mission above his own career."

"Listen to the quietest person in the room."

"The collective wisdom of a team is always greater than the ideas of one manager."

"To be a great leader, you don't have to have all the answers, but you need to have the right questions."

Questions to Ponder

1. Who are the future leaders in your organization? What can you do to provide challenging stretch assignments to showcase their skills and evaluate their potential?

2. Think about how you delegate. Are you more likely to delegate authority or responsibility? Based on your new understanding of these terms, what changes should you make to your leadership style in the future?

3. Name a time when you challenged a team and were surprised by their ingenuity and creativity. How can you foster more of this?

4. What would you consider an impossible goal in your business or industry? What would happen if you challenged your team to do it?

Chapter 8. Celebrate the Tough Times

The North Atlantic is a cruel and unforgiving body of water.
– Thomas Barnhart, Chief of the Boat, *USS City of Corpus Christi*

Winter in the North Atlantic

The winter seas in the North Atlantic were notoriously rough, but today they were absolutely brutal. The men aboard the 306-foot Edsall-class destroyer escort *USS Frost* were being tossed about like rag dolls. They were shaken but they remained on high alert. They stayed vigilant because their mission was far too important. The fate of millions of people in New York and Boston was in their hands.

In a last-ditch effort to turn the tide of the war, U.S. intelligence had discovered that Germany was plotting to send dozens of submarines armed with V-1 flying bombs to terrorize East Coast cities. The *Frost* was one of more than 20 destroyer escorts assigned to Operation Teardrop. Their job was to find and destroy these missile-armed U-boats before they could carry out their deadly attacks. Just before midnight on April 15, 1945, they made radar contact in the middle of a terrible storm.

A 23-year-old sailor gripped an electrical panel tightly as the ship pitched back and forth. This was his battle station on the *USS Frost*. His job was to ensure the ship's electrical systems remained fully functional while the ship made its attack. He heard on the 1MC that their sister ship, *USS Stanton*, had spotted a U-boat on the surface. The enemy boat was surfaced because it couldn't snorkel in the rough seas, which were later described as "mountainous."

The *Stanton* initiated an anti-submarine Hedgehog mortar attack against the surfaced boat, but somehow the submarine managed to submerge and escape. The *Frost* was now joining the fight in a desperate search for the evading submarine. The young sailor knew the hunters had just become the hunted. One well-placed torpedo would send the *Frost* and all of her 209 sailors to the bottom of the unforgiving Atlantic.

That sailor was my grandfather and that night his ship, the *USS Frost*, along with the *USS Stanton*, managed to overcome incredible odds. They found and sank not just one but two German submarines in the middle of a heavy storm. It was a tense battle that lasted the entire night but, in the end, the two destroyer escorts were able to outmaneuver and outgun the deadly U-boats. Both submarines suffered enormous explosions after being attacked, which reinforced the intel they were carrying missiles destined for the East Coast.

I had heard this story from my grandfather years ago – but I never imagined that 46 years later, at 23 years old, I would be on a submarine operating in the same area of the North Atlantic in a massive winter storm in a completely different war. As I gripped an electrical panel tightly to steady myself against the rolling seas, I thought about my grandfather and the dangerous situations he faced in the Navy during World War II. I was beginning to understand why he was the most calm and composed man I had ever known.

It was January of 1991, and I was on my first patrol on the *USS Tennessee*. Our operating area for this deployment was the North Atlantic. Our job was strategic deterrence and our enemy was the USSR. Our job was to remain undetected and be ready to launch our missiles if directed. Although significant changes were happening in Moscow, the Cold War was still in full strength and the Soviet fleet was desperate to locate us.

To say that winter storms in the North Atlantic are relentless is an understatement. To put it in perspective, the "perfect storm," made famous by the book written by Sebastian Junger and a movie starring George Clooney and Mark Wahlberg, would occur in the North Atlantic nine months after I made this patrol. That storm in October of 1991 contained 75 mph winds and hundred-foot waves. It killed 13 people, including the crew of the fishing vessel *Andrea Gail*.

As the newest officer on the *Tennessee*, I was still trying to get my bearings and learn the routines. The bad weather and the effect on the boat took me by surprise. I had no idea that a 560-foot submerged submarine would take this level of pounding 200 feet below the angry seas. We were taking rolls in excess of 30 degrees and the *Tennessee's* round hull offered no resistance to the swells. The fish tank in the wardroom had to be lowered to just a few gallons to keep it from sloshing out during the steepest rolls. Even the fish were miserable.

As I observed the crew, I could tell this wasn't normal. Seasickness was widespread, and even some of the most seasoned sailors were looking green around the gills. The cooks on the mess deck struggled to prepare meals in the heaving seas. They had to be careful not to allow pots and pans to crash to the deck, which could give away our position. I learned the importance of the phrase "rig for sea." This meant that everything had to be either tied or locked down to make sure it wouldn't come loose and fall to the deck during the heavy rolls.

My job this evening as the junior officer of the deck was to take the *Tennessee* to periscope depth and snorkel. This was part of my qualification process. Snorkeling was used to run the diesel generator at periscope depth. Many people are surprised to learn that nuclear submarines have diesel generators, but it is an essential piece of equipment. The diesel could be used to recharge the ship's batteries if there was a problem with the reactor, or it could be configured to ventilate a smoke-filled compartment in an emergency. Tonight was supposed to be a routine snorkel operation. It would be the first time I had ever taken the *Tennessee* to periscope depth, and it turned out to be a lot more than I ever expected.

We were rigged for red in control as part of the procedure for going to periscope depth at night. All the lights in control were set to red to make sure the officer of the deck and, in this case, the junior officer of the deck maintained their night vision before going to shallower depths. As I gripped the panel and looked at the team in control, what I saw was almost surreal. It looked like an animated version of a Hieronymus Bosch painting of hell. All of the sailors were cast in an eerie, monochromatic red hue as they pitched back and forth in the heavy seas.

I had been briefed on what to do and say to bring the ship to periscope depth, but I would first observe the officer of the deck do it. As the boat ascended, I noticed two things: (1) The seas became rougher and (2) we had trouble maintaining depth. The back of a Trident submarine is flat, and the heavy wave action across the boat caused the sub to get sucked towards the surface. I watched the diving officer and the chief of the watch struggle to keep the *Tennessee* at the proper depth without broaching. Broaching is a bad thing in the submarine world. It's when any part of the ship, other than the periscope, breaks the surface of the water. Broaching can lead to detection and, in the Cold War, detection was simply unacceptable.

After we returned to safer depths, the officer of the deck turned the watch over to me. It was my turn. I manned the periscope and began making quick sweeps with the optics pointed towards the surface as I had been taught. I looked for shapes and shadows, but all I could see was the dark ocean and an occasional bubble. When the scope broke the surface, I immediately looked for close contacts. What I saw was a chaotic cauldron of wind and waves that prevented me from doing a proper search. I made five complete sweeps before I felt confident enough to call out "No close contacts." It was at that point I noticed how bad this storm was. In the dim light of a cloudy sky with a waning moon, I saw the size of the waves. From the vantage point of the tiny periscope they honestly looked like mountainous.

Once the ship was ready to ventilate, I gave the command to raise the induction mast. This is a stubby mast on the back of the sail that contains both the intake and the exhaust ports for the diesel generator. There is a "head valve" at the top of the mast. This valve is spring-loaded shut and uses high-pressure air to stay open. There is a sensor on the mast that detects seawater. If water washes over the sensor, the head valve slams shut to prevent water from getting into the diesel. The valve is designed to prevent damage to the diesel and to prevent flooding. I was about to witness what happens when waves continually crash over this mast.

The plan was to stay at periscope depth for 15 minutes, run the diesel, then return to patrol depth. It sounded easy enough, but in these rough waters it proved to be extremely difficult. For the diving officer and chief of the watch, this was probably the longest 15 minutes of their lives. Every minute we snorkeled, they had to battle with the sea to stay shallow enough to allow the diesel to operate properly and deep enough to prevent broaching. It was a delicate operation made especially difficult in the unpredictable seas. I continued my periscope sweeps until another wave completely covered the scope. Then I heard it, the unmistakable sound of the head valve slamming shut.

Fortunately, the valve worked precisely as designed. It shut when the sensor was wet and reopened when the wave cleared. For the few seconds it was closed, however, the diesel continued to run, using the ship's air for intake and the ship's living space as an exhaust port. Yes, the diesel fumes ported directly into the submarine for those few seconds. One time might have been fine, but as we bobbed in the heaving seas and wave after wave passed over the scope, the head valve cycled open and shut countless times again.

At the end of 15 minutes the captain directed us to secure from snorkeling and return the ship to patrol depth. When we finally reached a safe operating depth, I lowered the scope and looked around control. As the lights came on, what I saw was surreal. A grey haze of fumes hung heavily in the space and everything smelled like diesel exhaust. Even those who weren't seasick before were now looking queasy. My stomach was doing somersaults as well. I had never felt this nauseous.

The team in control was battered and exhausted. The diving

officer, chief of the watch, helmsman, and planesman had just endured 15 minutes of intense concentration and effort to keep the *Tennessee* steady at periscope depth in the middle of this massive winter storm. There wasn't cheering or excitement to be back at a safer depth; the feeling was more like relief. The rolling seas at 200 feet now seemed pleasant compared to what we all had just gone through. Although I didn't know it at the time, this experience would profoundly affect my life.

After more than two weeks of operating in the North Atlantic's turbulent seas, the winter storm finally cleared and we experienced smooth sailing the rest of the patrol. In fact, in the six patrols I made after this one, I never experienced weather and ocean conditions even close to this. Those 16 days of being beaten and battered became my benchmark, my high-water mark. When things got bad, I would always remember that winter storm. That experience gave me a new perspective. I would recall what I went through and think, *This is nothing compared to my first patrol. I made it through that. I can make it through this.*

That's the interesting thing about tough times. They give you a new perspective. Your view of life forever changes from having withstood a difficult period. You have a much greater appreciation for when times are good. You are also less likely to let people and minor issues bother you. I think this is a big reason why my grandfather was so calm and composed. Nothing in his life ever came close to what he went through during the war. Every day he wasn't in a winter storm in the North

Atlantic being hunted by German U-boats was a good day. For me, it felt the same way.

Throughout my corporate career, my experiences as a naval officer made me look at problems differently from other people. Many called me an optimist because I never let the challenges we faced in business ever affect my confidence in our future success. When everyone was discouraged, I was always positive. It wasn't really optimism, though; it was perspective. Nothing I faced in business was ever as hard as taking a nuclear submarine to periscope depth at night in a winter storm. Those tough times at sea gave me a new perspective on land.

The important lesson here is that you should be encouraged if you are going through a rough patch in your life or business. It might be the best thing that ever happened to you. This situation may become your new high-water mark. As I have learned in my career, you truly learn to appreciate the storms in your life when they're over. I wouldn't want to go back and do it again, but I'm thankful that I experienced those two weeks in the North Atlantic. They helped me understand my grandfather so much more and gave me a new outlook on life.

THE YEAR WITHOUT A CHRISTMAS

It was a long watch in the engine room with not much going on. Like most watches, I had consumed my fair share of black coffee to stay awake and alert just in case something did happen. Thankfully, it was quiet and I was happy to turn over the watch when my replacement came into maneuvering. I headed up to the wardroom for lunch and to catch up with the other officers. What I saw when I opened the door evoked an emotional response I wasn't expecting.

My fifth patrol on board the nuclear submarine *USS Tennessee* started just like every other patrol. Once we left port, we were gone for months at a time with little contact with the outside world. We lived in complete isolation, and while it was never easy to be away from home, after five patrols I was getting used to it. I always found it was best not to think about what I was missing. However, like every other sailor on board, I still looked forward to the occasional "familygram" from home.

A familygram is a short, personal, one-way message of 50 words sent to submarine sailors on patrol from their families. Each sailor received one of these messages every two weeks or so. It was our only connection to what was happening at home, and the messages weren't even private. Each familygram was screened by Navy personnel, both when they were sent out and received, to ensure no bad news reached the deployed sailors. Aside from these heavily screened biweekly snippets from home, we were pretty much in our own little world.

What made this particular patrol unique was that our deployment went right through Christmas and New Year's Eve. It was evident when the captain first announced the patrol schedule that this one would be different. None of us would be home for Christmas this year. He reminded us that strategic deterrence was a 24/7 business and these holidays were just another day for us to do our job and "keep the peace." For most of us, this would be our first Christmas away from friends and family.

Being deployed over the holidays was affecting everyone differently. We each had unique family situations back home. Some sailors had young children and would miss seeing the joy on their faces as they opened presents on Christmas morning. Others had older parents and grandparents who didn't have many Christmases left. Those sailors would miss out on creating precious memories with their loved ones. I was newly married and would miss celebrating my second Christmas with my wife, but she planned to spend it with her parents; I knew she wouldn't be alone for the holiday.

When I walked into the wardroom that afternoon, I was surprised. It was two weeks before Christmas, and someone had hung dozens of strands of colored Christmas lights across the ceiling of the wardroom. The lights bathed the room in multicolored hues. For the first time on this patrol, I came face-to-face with my emotions. The tiny lights were a reminder of what I would be missing this year. For 25 years of my life, seeing Christmas lights had brought joy. Now they evoked another emotion – one which I had been avoiding this whole patrol. The lights made me homesick. As I looked around the table, I knew I wasn't the only one.

When I sat down to eat lunch with my fellow officers, I noticed something was different. The lights in the wardroom had changed things not just physically but emotionally as well. We were all feeling the same tug towards home. And the conversation during the meal turned to what we all would be missing this year. Favorite dishes, family traditions, and stories from Christmas past became the subjects of the conversation. The lighting change brought us all together, and we talked about the things we all were feeling individually.

Christmas under the Atlantic Ocean was going to be different for all of us. We knew the supply officer had planned a special meal for Christmas Day, and our families had each given us a box with small gifts to open. But it wouldn't be the same as being home. Despite the feelings we had, we each knew this was just part of the job. We knew there would be sacrifices when we signed up to be a submariner. Our boat's mission was important and necessary. We weren't the first sailors to miss Christmas and we wouldn't be the last. It was our turn. We had the watch.

When Christmas day arrived, it was just like every other day at sea. I got up early and stood my six-hour watch as EOOW in the engine room. After that I went up to the mess decks to see what was going on. I was surprised to see the extent of the meal the cooks had prepared for us. We had been at sea for well over a month. The meals had become somewhat routine and predictable, but today was truly special. There was a wide variety of traditional Christmas foods and desserts that had been carefully stowed away and prepared for this occasion. The cooks even roasted an entire pig for the crew in the ship's tiny galley. To this day I'm still not sure how they pulled that off.

After our Christmas meal the officers gathered in the wardroom, where we had dessert, opened gifts from our families, and talked about holiday traditions. We were a diverse group from all over the country, and it was fascinating to hear all the stories. We were each missing our families back home but we had each other, which made it bearable. In fact, that Christmas we all became a lot closer.

That's the thing about tough times. When you share them with other people, you build strong bonds. Standing shoulder-to-shoulder with others through a challenging situation creates relationships that can last a lifetime. That's because you face the challenges together. As you work together and suffer together, you build a shared experience. You also get to know your teammates better. On that patrol, I developed a new level of trust and appreciation for the people around me. I knew my shipmates had my back even in the worst times. The bond of mutual respect that formed on that patrol is hard to describe. None of us will ever forget that Christmas at sea.

I've had similar situations like this throughout my career where

I worked together with a team to overcome a difficult situation. In every case I built deep and lasting relationships with the people who were in the trenches with me. There's no doubt that you create strong bonds during tough times, and those bonds are tough to break. It's also true that the harder the challenge is, the tighter the bonds will become. If you are going through a period of difficulty, look to your left and your right. These are the people who will be with you through thick and thin. These are the people who will have your back.

Reactor Maintenance

The reactor compartment temperatures were hot but bearable for the amount of time each sailor would be in there. The radiation levels had finally dropped to the point where we could do the work safely. The part we had to replace was located right on top of the reactor. We would conduct the work in shifts. I stood at the command post outside the decontamination station and looked at my team. The final briefing was complete, and they were all now wearing EABs and donned in yellow anti-contamination suits (also known as "Anti-C's" or "canary suits").

Even through the masks, I could tell they were nervous. They had never done anything like this. In fact, no one had ever done this procedure on the East Coast before. I couldn't tell if they were just anxious about the job or worried about being led by a young, unqualified officer who just completed his first patrol. Even though I had spent a month preparing for this day, I still worried about what could go wrong. This procedure was the most dangerous and challenging thing I'd ever attempted in my 23 years on earth. I just hoped I had thought of everything.

This situation was the toughest test I faced as a new leader. I was leading the reactor controls team in a major maintenance activity after returning from my first patrol. We were replacing an instrument that failed during deployment. It was no easy task. It would require a sizable team to work in shifts to minimize heat and radiation exposure. It was a dangerous job and there wasn't much detailed information on how to do it safely.

As soon as the instrument failed at sea, I knew the responsibility to fix it would fall on my department and me. The pressure was on. The ship's engineer, my boss at the time, directed me to find out everything I could about the repair. I needed to learn what parts were needed, what tools were required, how long it would take, and how to test the instrument after it was installed. It meant digging through books, manuals, schematics, and maintenance procedures to find all this information. There were no helpful YouTube videos because YouTube hadn't been invented yet. Google was still seven years away from being created as well.

It took me weeks of late nights and early mornings to assemble the necessary information for the repair. However, it still wasn't enough to develop a detailed work procedure for this complex task. When we returned from patrol, I talked to the squadron and the engineers on the other East Coast boats. As it turned out, no other boat on this coast had ever made this repair. There was no precedent in the Atlantic fleet for what we were about to do. Fortunately for me, I discovered this procedure had been used in the Pacific fleet, so I started making phone calls.

After countless dead ends, I finally found the boat that had made this repair. It wasn't exactly the same instrument as on our boat, but it was the one right next to it. Discovering this was a breakthrough. I could use their maintenance procedure as a foundation to build ours. Using the research I had done and the West Coast information, I developed a detailed work procedure that included everything from parts and personnel to tools and timing. I meticulously spelled out every detail in this document. But that was just the beginning.

The chain of command had to vet the maintenance procedure thoroughly, and I had to order all the replacement parts. I also had to train each sailor to know his role and what to do if anything went wrong. Like directing a Broadway show, I had to choreograph every move by each operator. The time each sailor spent in the reactor compartment was purposefully short. I would have to monitor the temperature and radiation continuously and carefully control the tools. Each tool would be logged in and out of the reactor compartment so that nothing would be left behind. This maintenance activity was an arduous operation with severe consequences.

When the time came to conduct the operation, I set up my command post outside the decontamination station. Like a football coach, I had a clipboard that contained all the procedures, a stopwatch, and a phone operator who would be in constant contact with the sailors in the reactor compartment. I called all the plays as the yellow-clad operators entered and exited the compartment with tools and replacement parts. I tightly controlled every activity, and everything was going according to plan. The old indicator came out as expected and, to my relief, the new one was a perfect fit. So far there were no surprises.

After several tense hours the job was complete. Everyone was decontaminated and the hatch to the reactor compartment was dogged shut. We had successfully replaced the instrument and we accounted for all the tools. More importantly, every sailor was safe. We successfully became the first East Coast Trident boat to conduct this complicated maintenance procedure without incident. Now our equipment was back to full capacity.

For me, this was the most challenging project I had ever led. It cemented my role as the reactor controls team leader and a respected member of the crew. The ship's engineer and the rest of the officers knew I could be counted on to lead difficult tasks with proficiency. They saw the long hours and sleepless nights. They knew I had taken ownership from the beginning and saw this demanding task through to the end. This experience became an anchor point for the rest of my career in the Navy and beyond. I learned a lot about myself and what I was capable of from this time in my life.

I learned that tough times provide valuable experiences. They require you to operate at your highest level. When the seas are calm and the weather is nice, you don't have to be on the top of your game. But tough times require an intense, 24/7 focus on the problem. Everyone in the organization is depending on you to make the right decisions to lead them through the storm. It requires focus, determination, decisiveness, courage, intensity, and perseverance. In short, it takes your absolute best.

You learn a lot about yourself during tough times. The challenge of leading during a stressful period is learning to deal with those voices of self-doubt and worry while your team is depending on you for confidence and strength. Tough times are the ultimate test of a leader's character and resolve. Nothing will boost confidence more than facing the most formidable challenge in your life and coming out on top.

Great leaders can almost always point to a time in their career when they became great. In most cases, it was leading an organization through a challenging situation. The most difficult problem you face may be the defining moment in your career. For me, this experience became an anchor point. Thinking of this project always reminded me that I was capable of completing any difficult assignment. And that reminder stayed with me throughout the rest of my naval career and even into the business world. This project gave me confidence in my ability to get things done against the most challenging odds.

The Business World: Strike Team

As we drove by, my passenger started laughing. I turned to look and saw it as well. By this time, I was used to it. I had been called every name in the book and given the finger more times than I could count. But this gesture was truly epic. If insults were art, this would be considered a masterpiece. I turned in enough time to see an angry 60-year-old man with his legs shoulder-width apart, knees bent, giving me the two-fisted bird. I couldn't hear exactly what he was saying because the windows were up, but it sounded like "Fudge you!" I may have been mistaken, though.

Driving through the picket line had become routine at this point. We were involved in a prolonged labor dispute and I was stuck right in the middle. I was the vice president and general manager of this operation, but I wasn't the one calling the shots. The chairman of the board of the company I worked for was. He insisted the union needed to pay a portion of their healthcare costs. The union, of course, wanted no part of it. They had a rich benefits package and they weren't going to give it up. This issue was the hill they had decided to die on. They weren't backing down, so they went on strike. To make matters worse, the chairman also ordered me to get the production levels back to what they were before the strike – no matter what it took. I was in a no-win situation not of my choosing.

None of the local management team wanted a strike. We had worked hard for years to build bridges between the production employees, the office employees, and management. It wasn't perfect but it was getting better. Previous leadership had embraced an "us versus them" approach, but we were trying to change things. We thought the contract negotiation would be an excellent opportunity to see where we were. Unfortunately, we had a new chairman, and he wanted to make a name for himself. He had heard about the upcoming negotiations and, without any discussion, he mandated our approach. In no uncertain terms, he made it clear that he wouldn't approve any contract that didn't have the union paying for part of their healthcare benefits cost.

We knew our hands were tied but still felt we could negotiate with the union on this issue. The salaried employees had been paying a portion of their healthcare costs for years, and we thought it was only fair for union employees to contribute as well. Everybody knew healthcare costs were rising and the union already had an excellent deal. We had plenty of other negotiating options to offer the union in exchange for their agreement on healthcare costs, and we had high hopes of reaching an agreement. I had no idea this would be such a hot-button topic.

Like most companies in our position, we did some preliminary planning for production if the union went on strike. But I honestly felt it was in vain. I knew there was no way we could run the plant without the production employees. The only solution to keep production running was to get an agreement the union was happy with and that our chairman would approve. We were threading a needle but I felt it was possible. All that changed when I got the first reports back from the negotiating team. The union said that they would not pay a dime for their healthcare benefits no matter what else we put on the table. My hope for a quick agreement was dead on arrival.

We held many sessions with the union leaders to explain why we needed their help with healthcare costs, but they wouldn't budge. This was their Alamo. Too many other unions around the country had lost these rich benefits and they knew it was a slippery slope. Once union employees started to pay for these benefits, they felt management would just keep asking for more. I could see their point but I also knew this was a non-negotiable issue for us as well. Sadly, we were running headlong into an impasse. Eventually, the union decided to strike.

When I told the chairman the news of the labor strike, he was angry at me. He was upset that I had not reached a quick agreement with the union. He couldn't understand why they wouldn't just agree to all our terms. I'm not sure if he had ever been in a union negotiation before, but he certainly showed little empathy for our situation. He directed me to start up the factory with salary employees and hire strikebreakers, also known as scabs, to replace the factory workers. He wanted the plant back to normal production levels immediately. Those were my orders so that's what I tried to do.

The first day we crossed the picket lines and entered the plant was stressful for everyone. We met in the corporate offices across the street and loaded into school buses for the journey. Everyone was on edge. I had warned the salaried employees not to say anything as we passed through the picket. The union employees didn't have the same instructions. The profanity-laced screams and chants filled the bus as we drove into the plant parking lot, and they grew louder as we unloaded into the plant.

The head of manufacturing engineering had developed procedures on how to run each piece of equipment in the plant. He also had assigned managers to oversee each area. To my surprise, he assigned me to lead an area as well. It was "all hands on deck" and I was in charge of the winding department. My job on the first day was to teach the accounting department how to run the 25 electromechanical winding machines in this area. I had never operated these machines either. It was the blind leading the blind.

When I met the accounting team in the winding department, it looked like a scene of some bad action movie. You know the type: There's a small group of soldiers who have to train a bunch of farmers to protect their village from an enemy who will be there in three days. I was asking accountants to do something they had never done in their lives. While they didn't have pitchforks like in the movies, they certainly had the look of farmers being taught how to shoot a gun for the first time. They were nervous and so was I. This was a recipe for disaster, and I was worried someone would get hurt. While it always seems to work out in Hollywood, this was real life and it appeared hopeless. On day one we manage to produce precisely nothing.

In fact, for the first two weeks the salaried employees managed to produce about as much product as the union employees produced in an hour. It was discouraging. We were all exhausted and stressed from having to work in this strange new environment. Everyone was sore from standing on the concrete floors all day, and the union employees continued to harass us. We were all out of our comfort zone. I knew I had to do something to raise the spirits, so I started having morning meetings in the corporate offices before our daily drive across the picket lines. From that point on things began to get better.

In those morning meetings I would let all the salaried employees know what was going on that day. I would review the previous day's production numbers and remind people to stay safe and take their time. These daily meetings worked to get everyone on the same page. We were still in a challenging situation, but at least we all knew we were in it together. Every day the production numbers got a little better. Every day we celebrated because we were moving the needle. We were all excited because this ragtag group of salaried employees was running the plant safely and getting better every day.

Week after week, month after month, this went on until, with the help of strikebreakers, we eventually hit our daily production numbers. We were doing it! We were delivering the unexpected and we were having fun as well. The spirits in the shop were good. There was laughter, along with jokes and humor, throughout the plant. The morning meetings became a celebration of the previous day's performance. More importantly, no one got hurt. Everyone was taking their time and staying safe. We were all in a tough situation but managed to thrive even in this pressure-packed environment.

The strike went on for more than six months, and eventually cooler heads prevailed. We finally reached a deal and the union employees returned to work, which made me happy. It had been a long six months. To my surprise, many of the salaried employees didn't want to see the strike end. The strike had brought us closer as a team. The difficulties we faced together built deep bonds between all of us. We all learned we were far more capable than we realized. We each had operated at our highest level in the past six months, and we had achieved the unimaginable. This group of untrained office employees figured out how to run a complex manufacturing operation and bring production levels back to normal. And not one of the salaried employees was hurt during those six months.

That was my proudest accomplishment.

When I look back, I'm so glad I went through that difficult period. It gave me a new perspective. I matured as a leader and learned a lot about myself in the process. Nothing I did as a leader after that strike was as difficult as that. I was presented with the leadership challenge of a lifetime and I was able to deliver. My confidence as a leader skyrocketed, and I knew I was capable of much more than I ever thought.

Most of us don't want to go through difficult times. It's human nature to want things to be easy. The problem is that when things are easy and you aren't challenged, you don't grow. Confidence and maturity as a leader come from dealing with your self-doubt and fears while overcoming adversity. I'm glad I was able to lead such an amazing group of people for those six months. I will never forget those with whom I stood shoulder-to-shoulder during that difficult period. I wouldn't want to do it again, but I'm thankful for the experience and the lessons I carry even now.

Middle of Patrol

After lunch I headed back to the engine room. Even though I had just spent six hours there on watch, I still had to do my job as the reactor controls officer. I was going aft to meet with my chief petty officer to discuss the weekly preventive maintenance schedule. We had to complete dozens of maintenance activities on the reactor instruments each week. My job was to coordinate those tasks with the ship's engineer.

As I was looking for my chief, I decided to stop by maneuvering and talk to my buddy, Sam. He was the EOOW for the afternoon watch. "Request permission to enter maneuvering," I said as I stood outside the starboard door.

"Enter," Sam said groggily.

"Enter, aye," I said as I moved the chain and entered the cramped space. As I looked around, I saw all the familiar panels and gauges I had just been staring at for the last six hours. Nothing had changed. I also saw the same expressions on the faces of all the watchstanders. This team was just as bored as we were on the last watch.

"Hey, Sam," I said. "How's it going?"

"How's it going? Dude, I'm rottin' in the box. That's how it's going."

Sam always had a colorful way of putting things but his description was accurate. Standing watch in the engine room in the middle of the Atlantic Ocean on patrol was often routine and uneventful. Once we were in our patrol areas, our mission was to slow down, be quiet, and remain undetected. We made slow circles in the ocean, going five knots to nowhere. We had a funny expression for it as well – "hide with pride." And after hiding with pride for two months with no end in sight, things got pretty dull. Many people think life on a submarine is exciting. While there certainly is a lot of excitement, most days on patrol were pretty ordinary. The old military adage best describes life on a missile boat on deterrent patrol – "months of boredom punctuated by moments of terror."

I was cleaning out some old boxes in our attic recently and found a letter I wrote to my future wife from this very patrol. It gives you a sense of what life was really like on the boat:

> *All is well out here in the middle of the Atlantic. Flipper and Orca send their best. We've gotten ourselves over the hump, and now it's all downhill from here. At this point in the patrol, drills seem easy, the captain's temper seems mild, and day-to-day life seems pretty normal to us – even though we're out here just making circles in the ocean, protecting Mom, hot dogs, baseball, and apple pie from the threat of the Communist hoard.*

Our job on patrol consisted of doing the same difficult tasks every day for months at a time until they became routine, easy, and even boring. But those countless hours of work in the middle of deployment developed our persistence, and they allowed us to become more competent in our jobs. Tough times aren't always about overcoming a difficult situation. Many times it's just doing the long, challenging, and often dull work necessary to achieve an important goal. If you're an entrepreneur, you know what I mean.

There is excitement when you first open your company, but the hard and often tedious work comes months after the excitement wears off. Still, those long periods of persevering through the day-to-day work of building a business are essential in developing your character and competence. As is always the case, the real work, effort, and growth come in the middle.

In Donald Miller's book, *A Million Miles in a Thousand Years*, he talks about the importance of the struggle in the middle of doing anything important. He said:

> *The reward you get from a story is always less than you thought it would be, and the work is harder than you imagined. The point of the story is never about the ending, remember. It's about your character getting molded in the hard work of the middle.*

As Miller suggests, the hard work in the center of any difficult challenge is more important than the ending. The struggle develops persistence. The ninth mile of a half-marathon race crossing a bridge in the cold, windy, pouring rain is when we find out who we really are. (Yes, that happened to me.) We learn we can achieve amazing things if we just don't quit.

Angela Duckworth, the author of *Grit: The Power of Passion and Perseverance*, defines grit as passion and perseverance for long-term goals. She explains that grit is about having "a goal you care about so much that it organizes and gives meaning to almost everything you do. And grit is holding steadfast to that goal. Even when you fall down. Even when you screw up. Even when progress toward that goal is halting or slow." On the *Tennessee*, our ultimate goal was to protect our country. We all knew what we were doing required sacrifice. We volunteered for this duty because we each had a deep passion for our country and we wanted to do our part. Enduring months away from home doing dangerous work was just part of the job. We persevered because the long-term goal was too important not to.

Over time, the struggle changed us as well. The months of hard work during patrol molded our character. The challenge brought about change. As we powered through countless hours of underwater life, we developed character strengths like persistence, resolve, and resilience. Often it took everything we had to keep going, especially when the end of patrol seemed so far away. But that's when the experience shaped our character the most. We pushed through, knowing the goal was worth the sacrifice, and we became tougher in the process.

The hours, days, and months under the ocean developed a personal narrative of who we were and what we could accomplish. If you think about it, every great movie has a hero's journey. The main character must struggle and overcome a significant obstacle or challenge. As an audience, we become endeared to the hero as they face hardships and trials. It's the same with people who endure tough times. We all become more interesting when we have faced trials and overcome them. It's been said that a sailor is defined by how many storms he has overcome. We build a more fascinating story by having persevered through difficult times.

We also become more competent. In *Outliers: The Story of Success*, Malcolm Gladwell introduced the concept of the "10,000-Hour Rule." That rule states that the key to achieving world-class expertise in any field is by practicing the correct way for a total of around 10,000 hours. In seven patrols on the *Tennessee*, I spent more than 13,000 hours under the ocean. In the months of training, drills, and standing watch in all types of situations, I became a better submariner. I became more competent in my craft.

Not only was my character molded in the middle of a long patrol, but my proficiency grew and I sharpened my skills. I developed muscle memory and intuition. I could see things before they happened. I'll freely admit that it was often boring to do the same things for months at a time. But Bruce Lee had it right when he said, "I fear not the man who has practiced 10,000 kicks once, but I fear the man who has practiced one kick 10,000 times." There is no shortcut to building a high level of competency. If you want to be good at anything, you have to put in the work.

During those long deployments on the *Tennessee*, I learned that the hard work in the middle of any difficult challenge is life-changing. As Donald Miller reminds us, it's during these times that we mold our character. In my case, I learned the value of persistence, resolve, and resilience. I learned that if I could tolerate 13,000 hours in a metal tube under the sea, I could withstand much of what life could throw at me.

As an entrepreneur, this experience helped me endure the long days and typical setbacks of trying to start and build a new business. I handled adversity without giving up because I had a long-term goal that was far more important than the short-term pain. I persisted when others gave up because I had developed grit.

If you find yourself in the middle of a long-term struggle, celebrate the fact that you are in the right place. Yes, it's tough, but your current situation will shape your character and build your competency. You will also discover you are capable of much more than you thought possible if you just keep going and don't quit.

THE BUSINESS WORLD: A CRAPPY CUP OF COFFEE

Winter in northern Ohio is tough, and the people who live through these winters are even tougher. It was there when I realized my calling, when I knew what I wanted to do with my life.

As division vice president of a global industrial business, I was responsible for the manufacturing plant I was visiting in Ohio that winter. I was 35 years old and eight years out of the Navy. I had been in the manufacturing world ever since I left the Navy, but I was still trying to figure out exactly what I wanted to do with my life. I had fulfilled my dream to serve as a submarine officer and now I was a civilian. Like many veterans, I went to work for corporate America to pay the bills, but I didn't really have a plan. I never really thought of life after the military. I knew that at some point I would have to figure it out.

Three years earlier I had implemented monthly "all employee" meetings in my first plant manager role. I thought it was essential to communicate how the business was doing and the priorities each month. I also loved interacting with the manufacturing plant personnel. In a way, it was a lot like working with the sailors on the *Tennessee*. In my current position I was responsible for two manufacturing plants. In the middle of winter I had come to the Ohio plant to meet with the employees.

It was two in the morning when I left the hotel to drive up to the plant. It was a cold night and the lake-effect snow coming off Lake Erie was blowing hard. The snowbanks on each side of the road towered over my SUV as I slowly made my way to the industrial complex near the lake. The plan was to talk to the third shift team that night. I had to deliver some bad news and the rough weather only darkened my mood.

We had a room reserved right outside the production line on the second floor. The manufacturing building was old, dark, and drafty.

It was only slightly warmer than it was outside but at least I was out of the wind. Despite the frigid temperatures, I was still trying to wake up and I needed some coffee. I found a greasy old coffee pot on a table right outside our meeting room. I poured some hot, black coffee into a small Styrofoam cup and went into the meeting.

The plant quality manager was presenting the monthly quality numbers first, so I sat in the back of the room and listened. I was thinking about what I was going to say. This plant was losing money. We had to turn it around or upper management would shut it down. I wasn't sure how I was going to create a sense of urgency without inciting panic.

As I sat there and listened to the presentation, I looked down at my coffee. It was the worst cup of coffee I had ever seen in my life (far worse than anything in the Navy). Strange things were floating in it. There was a sheen of oil on the surface and I could see coffee grounds on the bottom of the cup. It was absolutely dreadful. But I was exhausted and drank it anyway. It was at that point when I realized my purpose in life.

With an engineering degree, two master's degrees, military service, and 13 years of leadership experience, I thought *I could be anywhere doing anything*. I could be working at a big company like IBM or General Motors, drinking a Starbucks latte, and doing incredible things in a fancy climate-controlled office. I didn't have to be in Ohio, in the winter, in an old drafty manufacturing plant, in the middle of the night, drinking probably the worst cup of coffee ever made. I didn't have to be in charge of a business losing money that needed a turnaround. But as I thought about it, I realized there was nowhere else I would rather be.

Despite the challenges (or maybe because of them), I wanted to be with these employees. I wanted to share what I knew about the state of the business. I wanted to work with them to craft a plan to turn the company around and become profitable. I wanted to lead these people and this business. I wanted to be here and nowhere else in the world. I wanted to make a difference and fight for the people at this plant.

Ernest T. Campbell of the Riverside Church of New York City said, "The two most important days of a man's life are the day on which he was born and the day on which he discovers why." That night I discovered my why. That crappy cup of coffee told me that I had found my life's purpose. I knew that, despite the challenging circumstances, I was built for this. I wanted to be here and lead this manufacturing team. This was my mission.

Over time, we turned this plant around. I hired an amazing plant manager who had the same passion for manufacturing employees as I did. He spent countless hours on the shop floor building relationships and figuring out how to get the most out of this old manufacturing facility. We worked together to fix the quality issues, improve on-time delivery, and eventually make money. By the time I left this role, the employees at that old plant by the lake were producing double-digit profits. That plant went from being a losing business to being a positive contributor to the company – all because a crappy cup of coffee helped me find my purpose.

In my experience I have found that tough times are like a refining furnace. They help reveal what you really want in life. In this case, the tough times facing this business helped me understand that I wanted to be part of the turnaround. I wanted to be there and help these employees. This was my purpose. I've had other situations where the pressure of a challenging situation told me just the opposite.

My last job in corporate America was working for a large multinational company headquartered in Europe. The European parent had acquired the U.S. operations in 1991. The once-proud American company had become subservient to its European masters. Morale was low, and the company was mired in bureaucracy and red tape. As a leader in this business, I spent nearly eight hours a day in meetings discussing issues that I knew would never get resolved. Local managers had very little autonomy and no authority to address problems without approval from upper management. No one was authorized to make decisions at the local level. Frustration and apathy ran rampant in the U.S. organization. Employee engagement was almost nonexistent.

As one of the senior managers at the site where I worked, upper management asked me to lead the annual strategic plan communication session, which happened every January. It was an event where the company's top managers talked about the goals for the year. It was actually a well-executed, multimedia event with both live and recorded videos for all employees. It was a perfect way for a top-down company to tell people what they wanted them to do.

Two weeks before the event I received a call from corporate saying they would be sending a gift for every employee at our site. I would be responsible for handing them out during the event. I was surprised and impressed that upper management took the time to do something special for the employees. That was, of course, until I received the package. Two days before the meeting I received a box from corporate with 600 buttons that said, "I love my job." I wish I were kidding! They wanted me to give these buttons to a workforce who was already frustrated and disgruntled. It was one of the most tone-deaf leadership moves I had ever seen in my life.

Like that crappy cup of coffee, those buttons were a wake-up call. They helped me find my true purpose. At the exact moment I saw the buttons, I knew I was finished with corporate life. It was abundantly clear that most large corporations don't really care about the people who work in the trenches. It was at that moment that I began thinking about starting my own business. It was time to escape corporate life. I wanted to be part of an organization where people were treated with respect – and I wasn't going to find it in my current job. My reaction to this tough situation was that it was time to go. My 22-year career in corporate America was over and I eventually left to become an entrepreneur.

The beauty of experiencing tough times is they bring clarity. They help you determine your real purpose. The added pressure and stress of a difficult situation serve to activate our fight-or-flight response. Through these experiences we can clearly see our next move. That night in Ohio I saw my purpose with clarity. I knew I wanted to stay and fight for the employees of that plant. The box of "I love my job" buttons help me realize my next move as well. I knew I had to leave.

If you are going through a tough patch right now, consider it a blessing. The added pressure of the circumstances you are facing will help you find your life's purpose. It will help provide the clarity you need to make the right decision for your future. Will you stay and fight or will you run? The choice is entirely up to you.

Celebrate the Tough Times

The Bottom Line

Key Points

- Tough times give you a new perspective.
- You build strong bonds during hard times.
- Adversity requires you to operate at your highest level.
- You learn a lot about yourself during difficult challenges.
- Enduring hard periods builds confidence and maturity.
- Tough times become the anchor point for the rest of your career.
- The hard work in the middle of any difficult challenge is life-changing.

Tweetable Quotes

Tweet the following quotes with these hashtags: #allinthesameboat #toughtimes

"Your view of life forever changes from having withstood a difficult period."

"Standing shoulder-to-shoulder with others through a difficult time creates relationships that can last a lifetime."

"When the seas are calm and the weather is nice, you don't have to be on the top of your game."

"Tough times require an intense, 24/7 focus on the problem."

"Tough times are the ultimate test of a leader's character and resolve."

"There is nothing that will boost confidence more than facing the toughest challenge in your life and coming out on top."

"The most difficult situation you face may actually be the defining moment in your career."

"Confidence and maturity as a leader come from dealing with your self-doubt and fears while overcoming adversity."

"A sailor is defined by how many storms he has overcome."

Questions to Ponder

1. What tough times have you faced in the past? What lessons did you learn from those experiences?

2. Are there situations you are avoiding because you know they will be difficult? What can you take away from this chapter to challenge your thinking?

3. Name one skill where you are highly confident in your abilities. Where did that confidence come from?

4. Who are the people you have stood shoulder-to-shoulder with in tough times? What is your relationship like today?

Afterword

Congratulations! If you have reached this point, you are part of an elite group: 85% of people who purchase a business book never read it. It just sits on their shelf like a trophy and collects dust. Of the 15% who do, only 25% make it beyond the first chapter. If you are here, you are in the top 3-4% of people who have purchased this book. But I want to challenge you. There is another level.

Even rarer still are those who both read *and* implement the ideas from a book. This is a special group of individuals. In the nuclear submarine officer training pipeline, only the best make it through their training and earn the right to wear submarine dolphins on their uniforms. I want to challenge you to push through to the next level as well.

Consider the stories that I presented in this book. Which ones stood out to you? Or, if you are like me, which sections have the most highlighting? Now, think about the reasons why. These particular stories are speaking to you for a reason. It doesn't matter where you are in your leadership journey you can always get better. Award-winning business author and executive coach John Brubaker likes to say that the best ideas come from *outside your industry*. Unless you are a fellow submariner, the stories in this book should be well outside your industry.

The questions are: Which of these ideas are you going to implement? And how will those concepts help you to become a more effective leader?

Now, don't just think about it. Do it.

The reason I wrote this book is to address the problems I see in business leadership today. I'm on a mission to build a world with better bosses. I don't just want readers; I want leaders. Right now there is a leadership crisis in most companies. Too many people are working in uninspiring jobs with unimpressive, self-centered bosses. We need *better* leaders. And the only way to get better is to take action.

Consider the motto of the U.S. Merchant Marine Academy: *Acta Non Verba* – actions, not words. I challenge you not just to ponder these ideas; put them in motion. Take advantage of your current inspiration and take action. If you want to become a leader worth following, you should constantly push yourself to get better. I hope the stories in the book inspired you to take the next step.

Reach out to me and tell me what you are working on. Tell me what stories sparked a change in your approach to leadership. Let me know how that change is making a difference in motivating your people to do extraordinary things. I encourage you to continue to seek self-improvement and never stop learning as you move through your leadership journey.

As we say in the Navy, I wish you *fair winds and following seas*.

Event Speaking and Group Training

It is one thing to study war and another to live the warrior's life.
- Telamon of Arcadia

If you want to step up your employee engagement with stories from the front lines of leadership, hire Jon to speak at your next event. Custom-tailored keynote speeches and training programs for your organization based on the principles of *All in the Same Boat* are available at:

JonSRennie.com/speaking

Coaching and Mentoring

Take your business or career to the next level. If you're a leader or business owner, think of yourself as a professional athlete. If you want to get to the top of your game, you need a coach, someone who has been in the game and reached the highest levels. Professional athletes hire coaches to give them an advantage over the competition. They look for people who have deep experience in winning. Hire Jon to help you get the most out of your career and company. More information is available at:

JonSRennie.com/coaching

Bulk Book Purchases

All of Jon S. Rennie's books can be purchased in bulk for large industry groups or your organization at a discount. Please contact customer service for more information at:

JonSRennie.com/connect

Also by Jon S. Rennie

An Amazon Bestseller!

"This book cuts to the heart of the matter of leadership: it's all about people."

Joshua D. Cotton, PhD, Founder and CEO, VetStoreUSA

Available for purchase at:

JonSRennie.com

About the Author

Jon is a business leader, author, podcaster, and speaker. He is co-founder, president and CEO of Peak Demand Inc., a manufacturer of critical infrastructure products for electric utilities. He served as a U.S. naval officer on nuclear submarines and has close to 30 years leading industrial businesses in North America.

The most important lesson he's learned during these years is that leadership matters. He knows that strong leadership can make a significant difference in the performance of any organization. He shares his thoughts and insights on business and leadership with a singular mission: to build a world with better bosses. His hope is that this book inspires you to look at leadership in a new light.

His leadership book, *I Have the Watch: Becoming a Leader Worth Following*, is an Amazon bestseller.

For more information visit:

JonSRennie.com